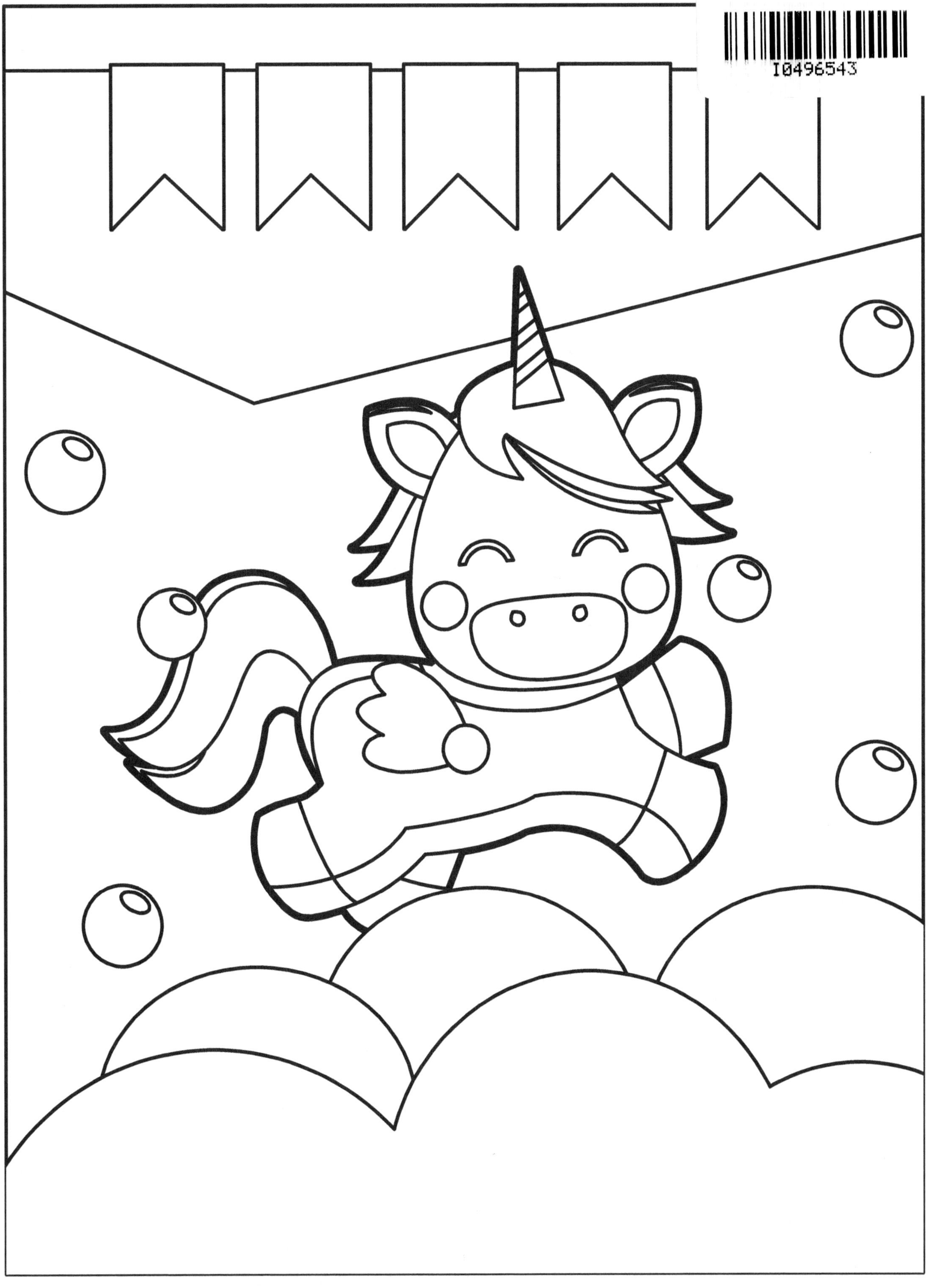

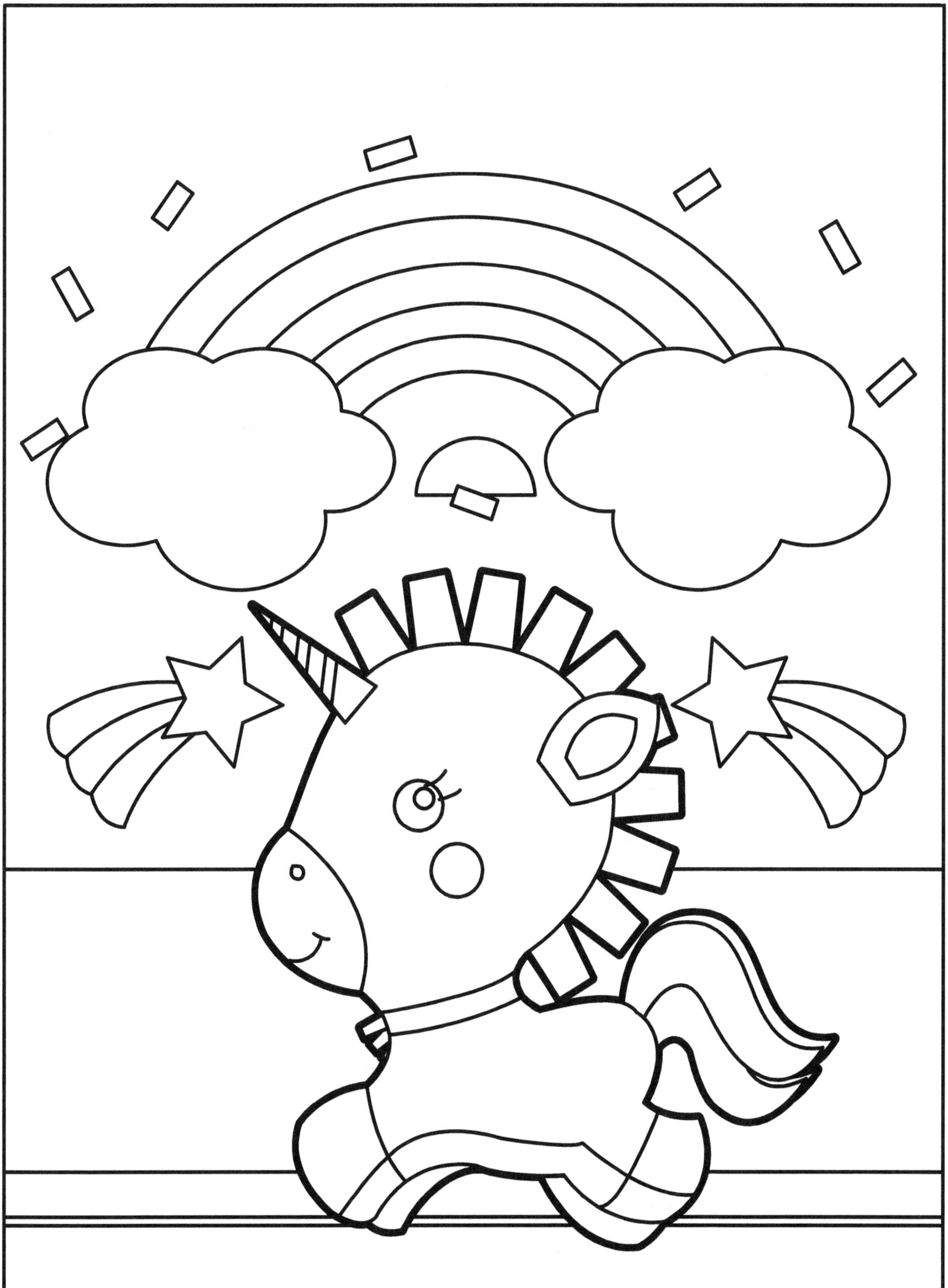

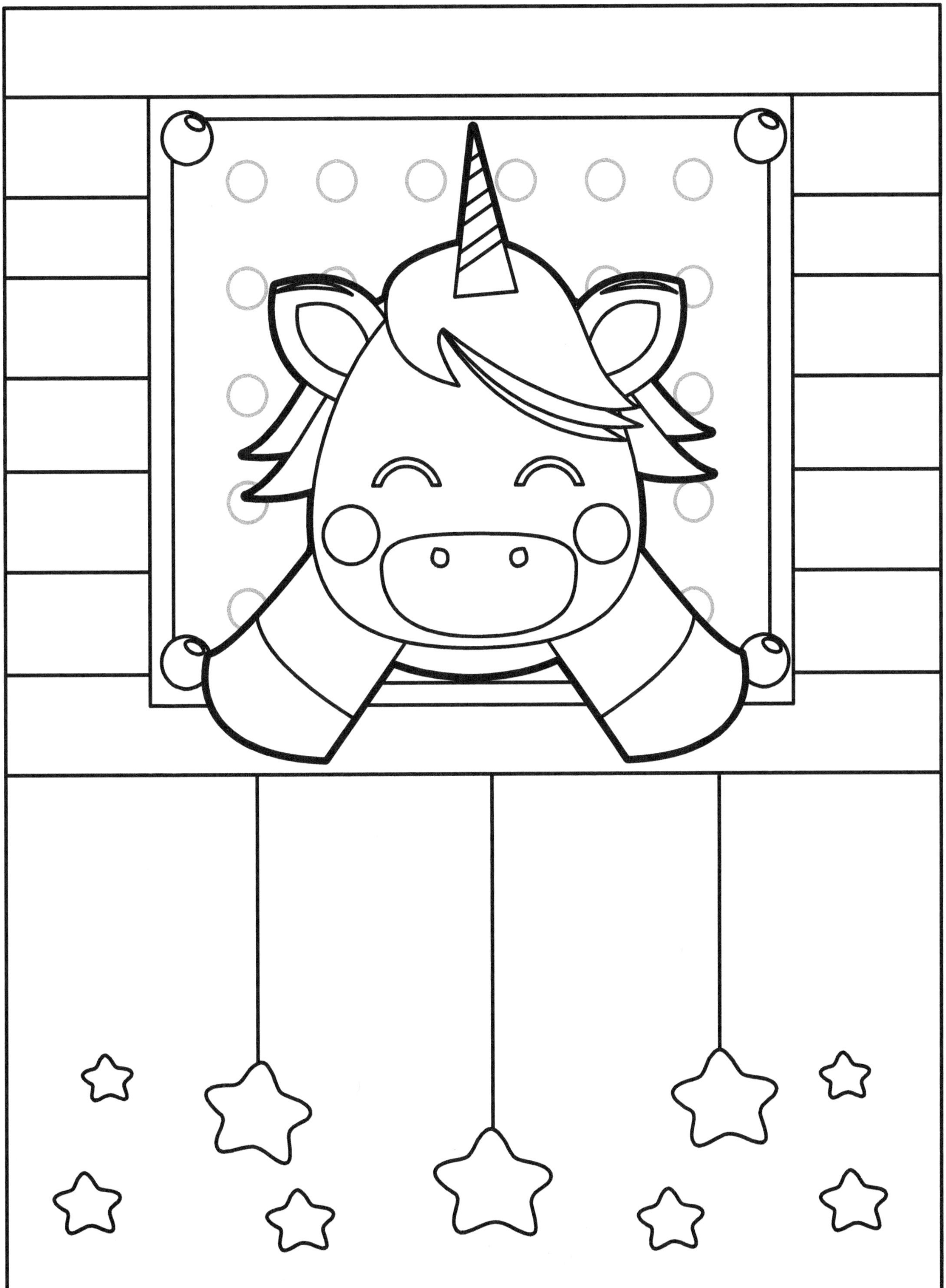

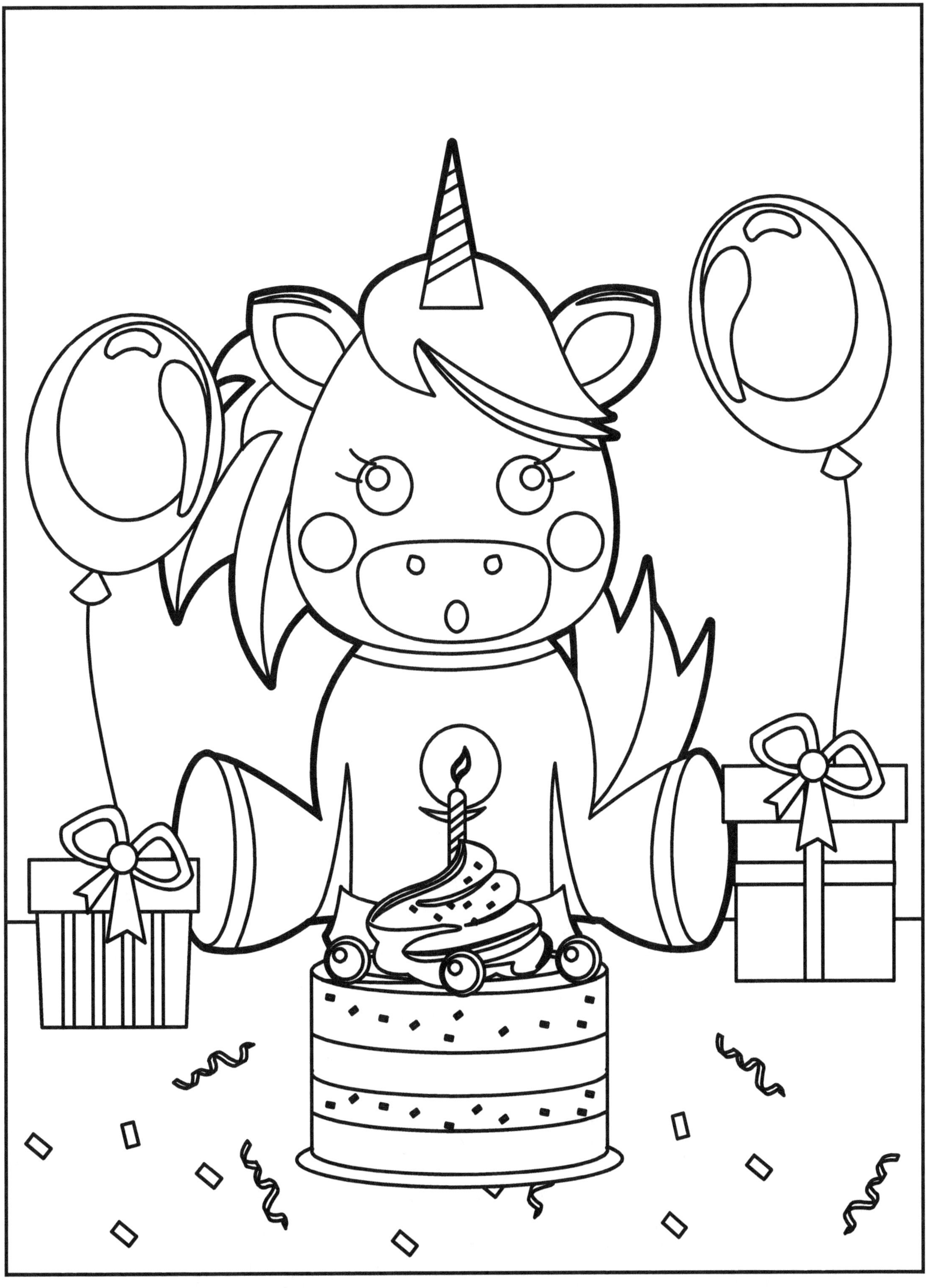

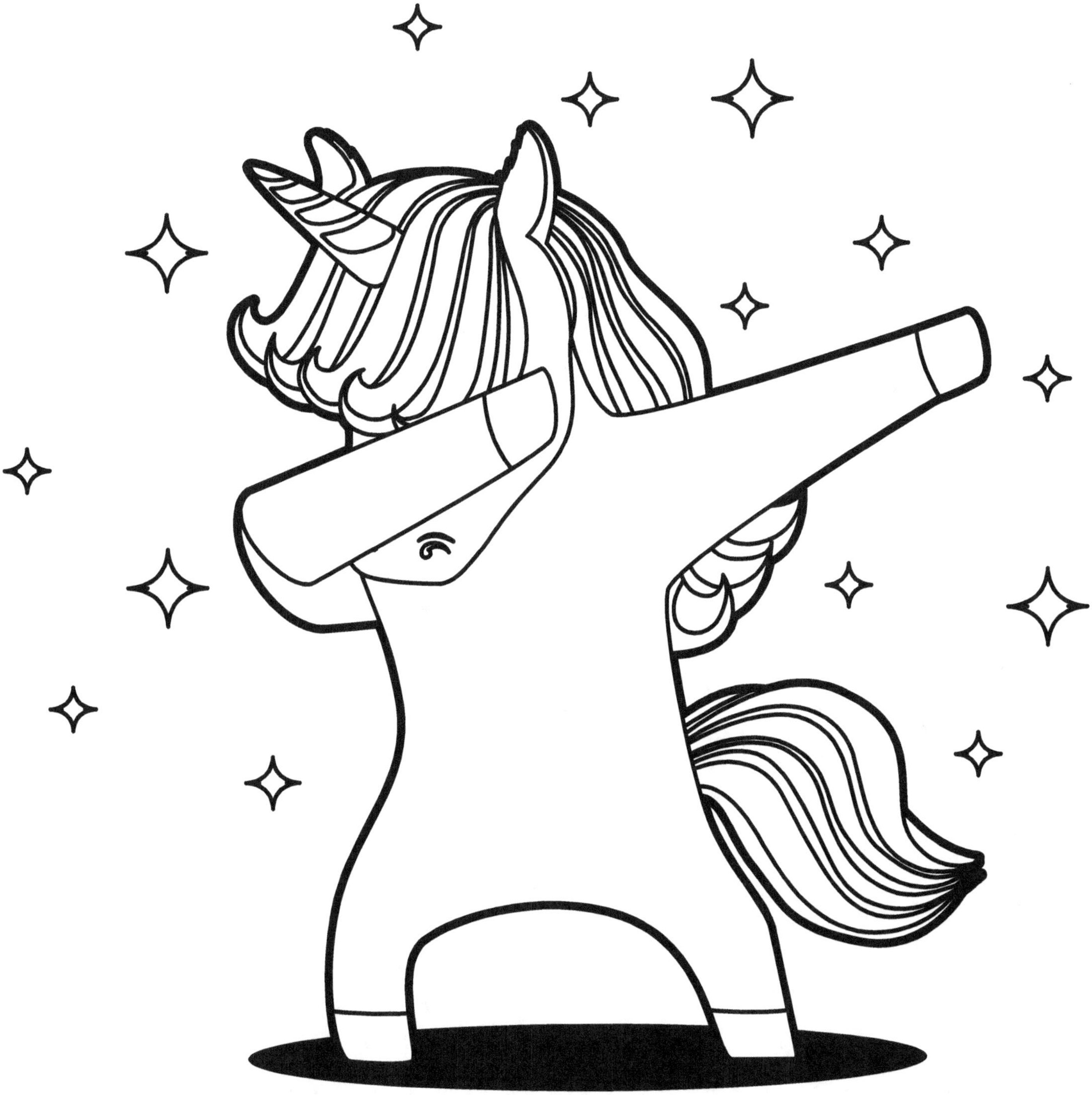

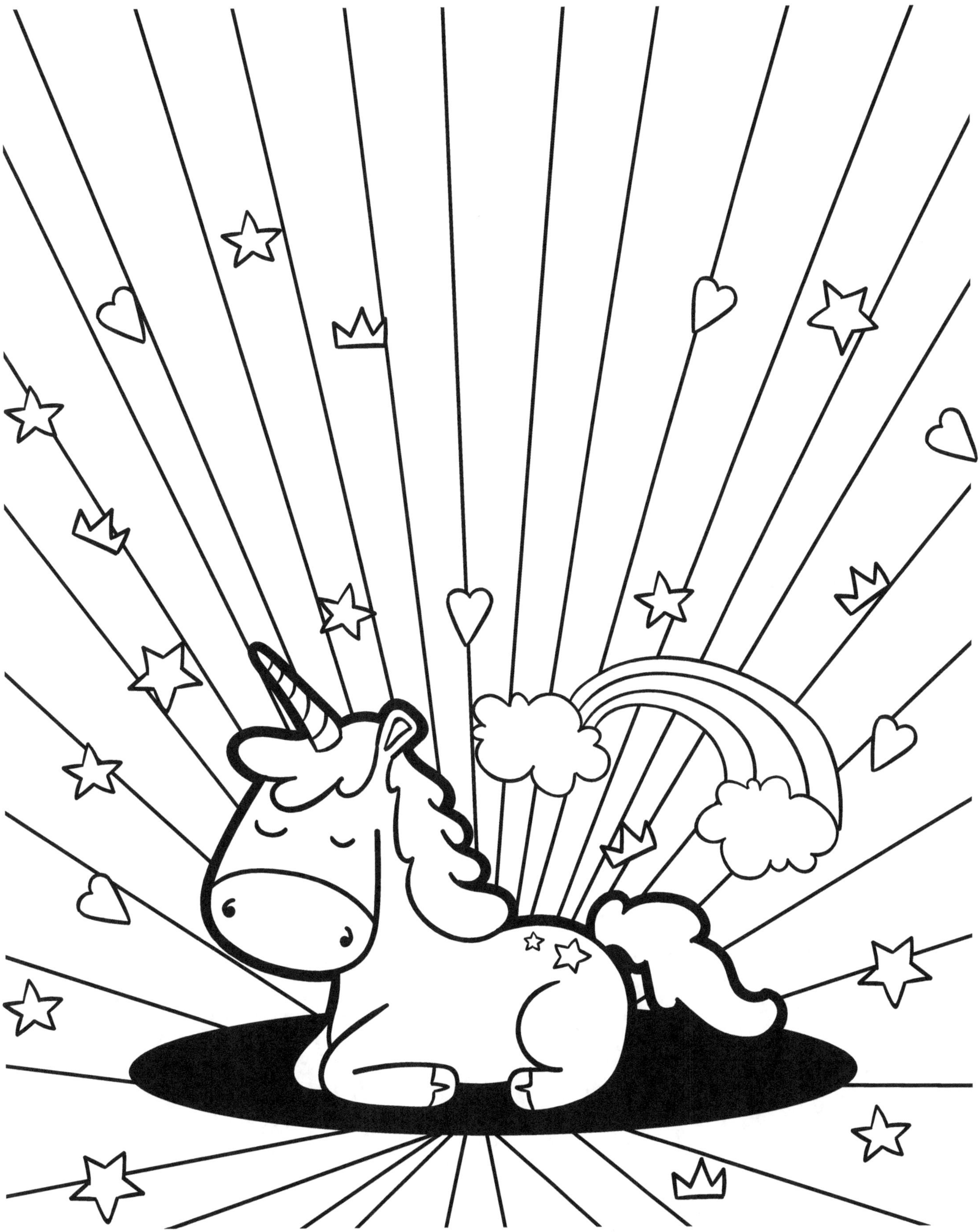

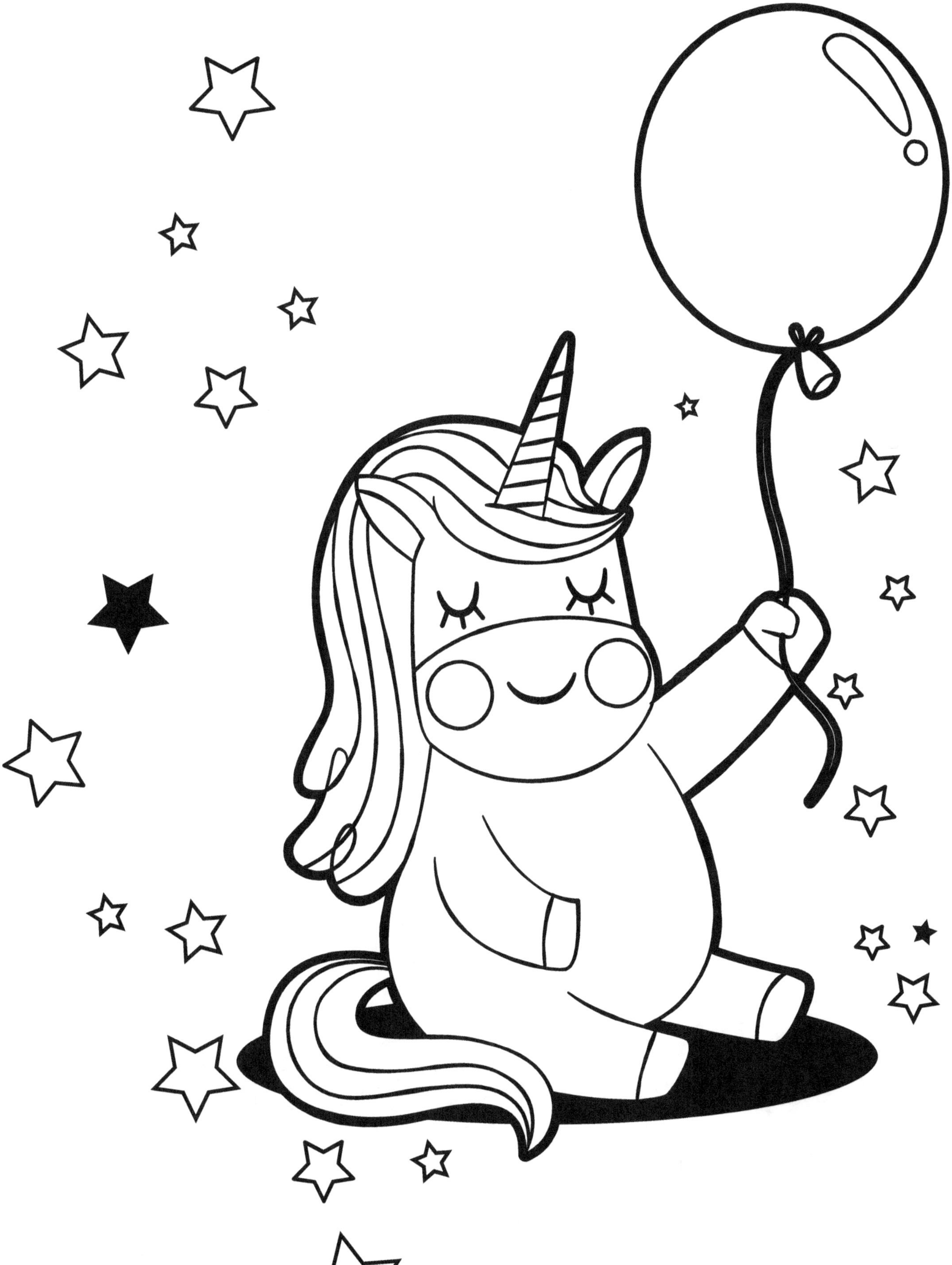

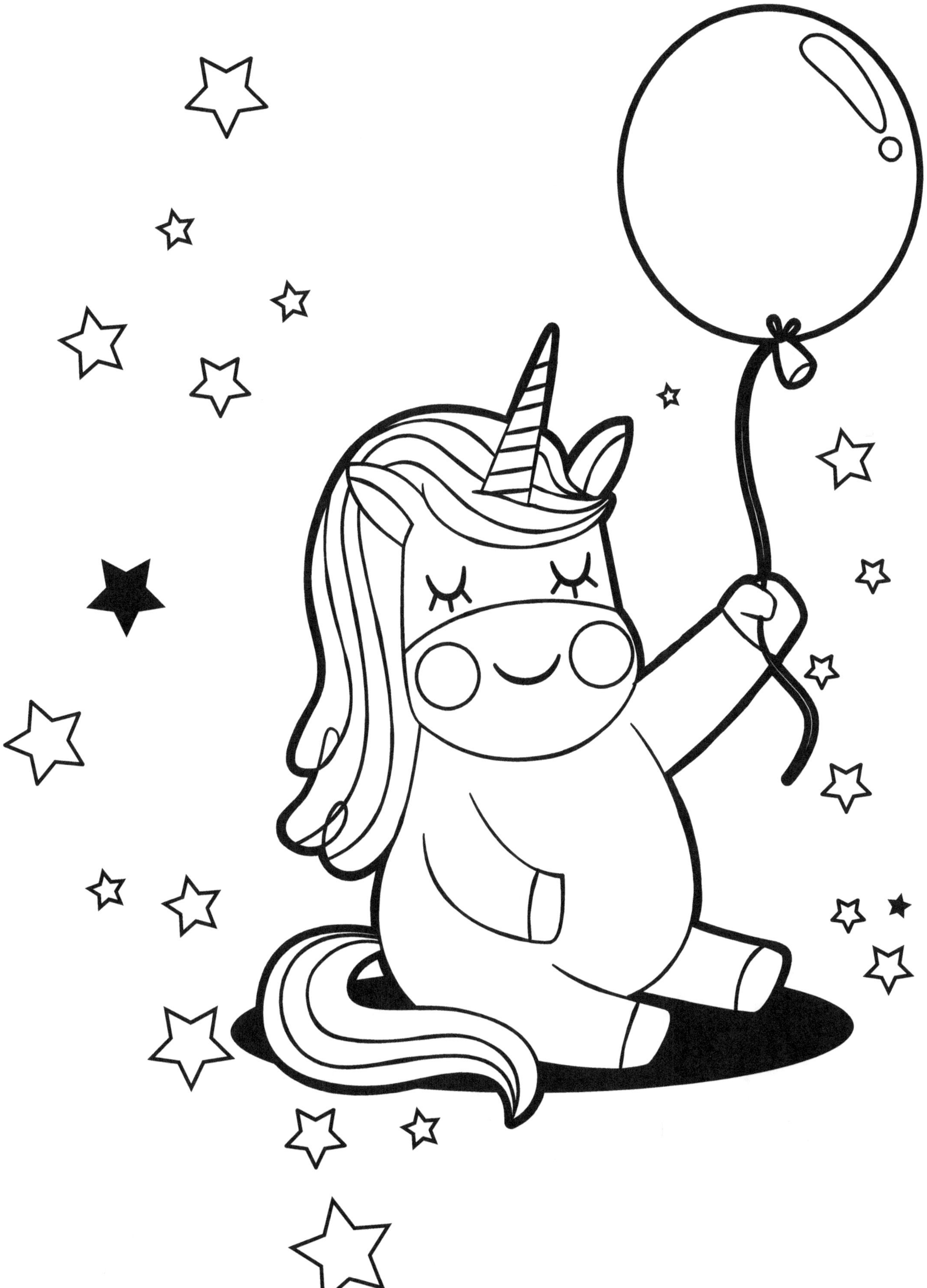

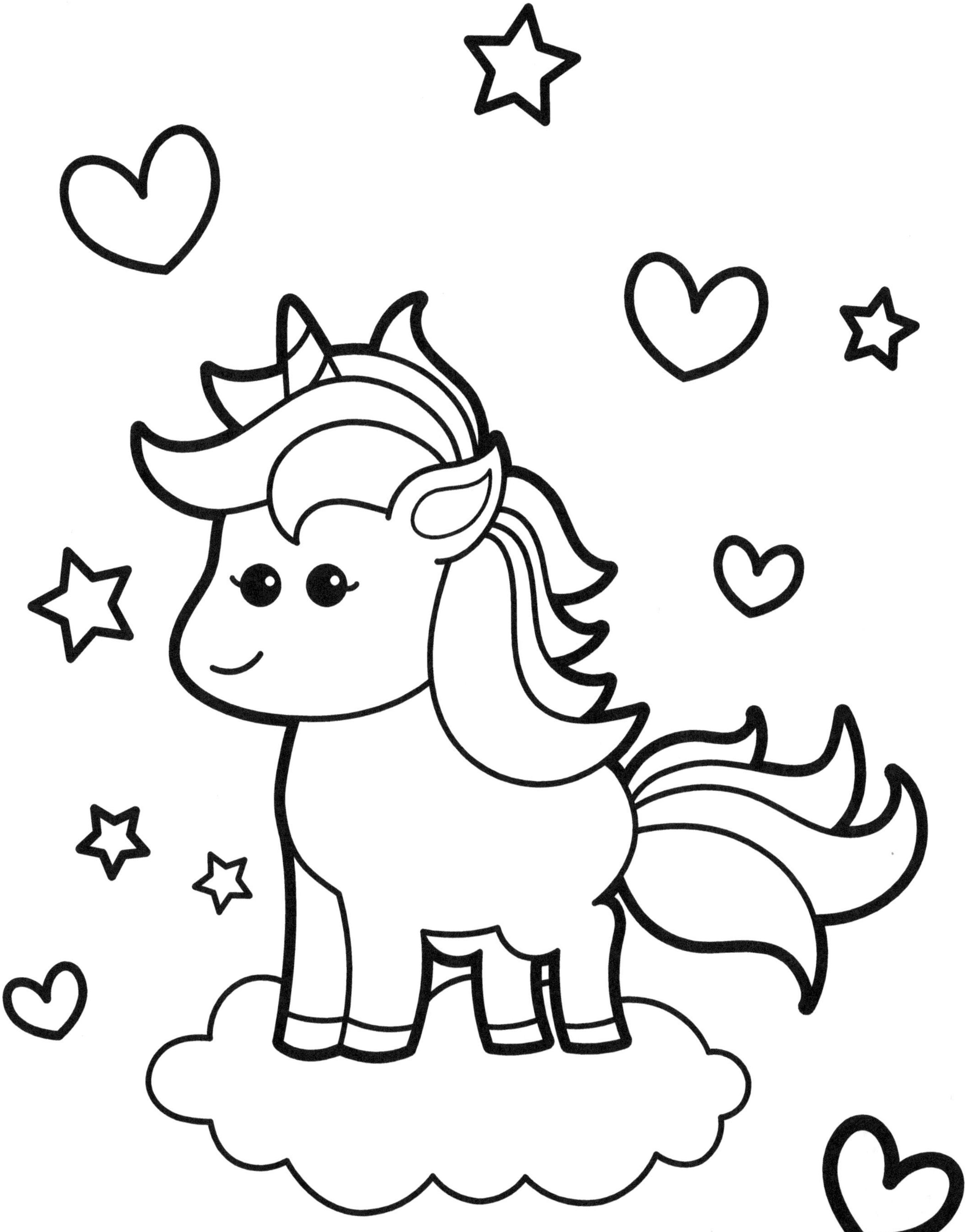

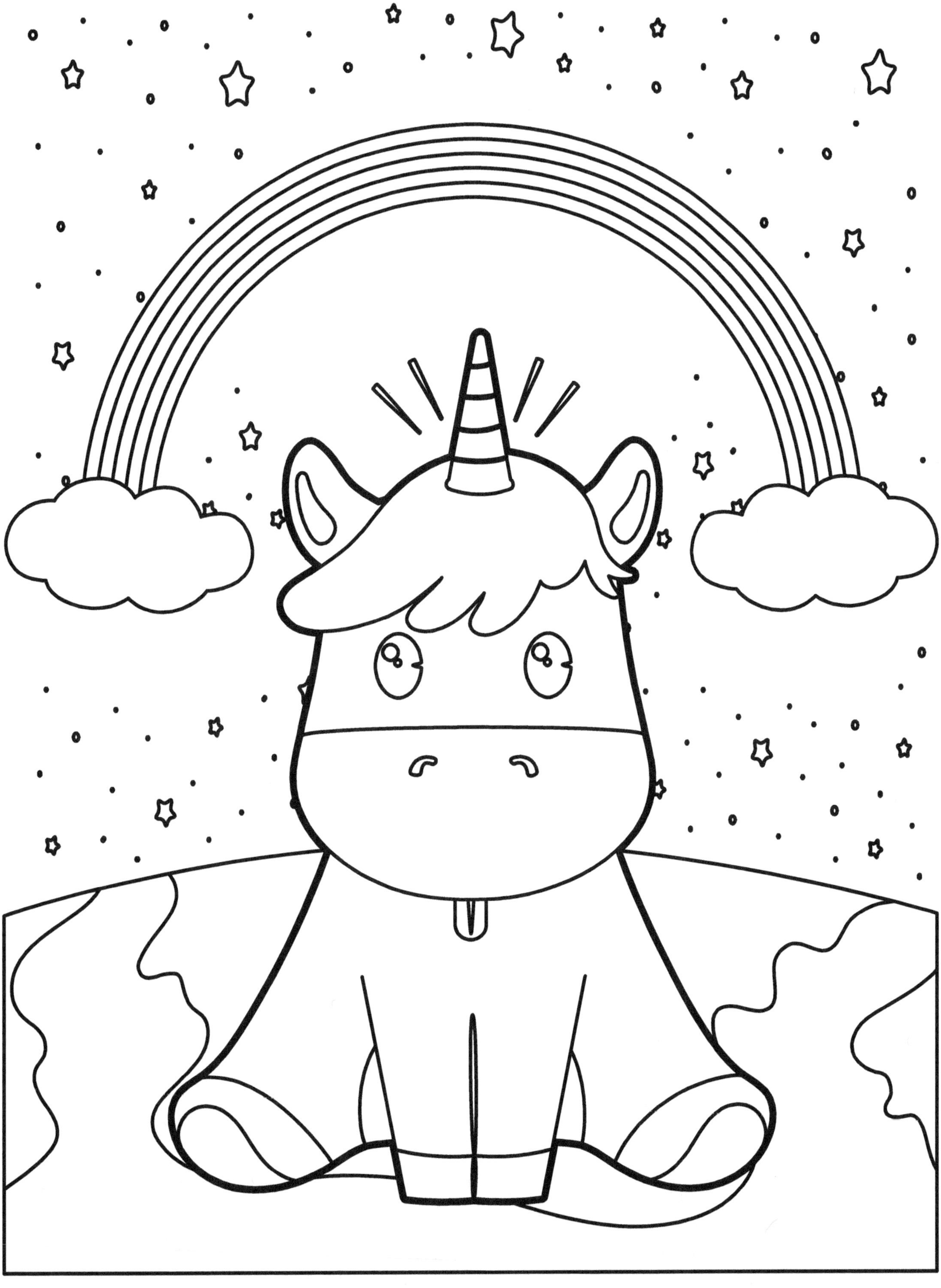

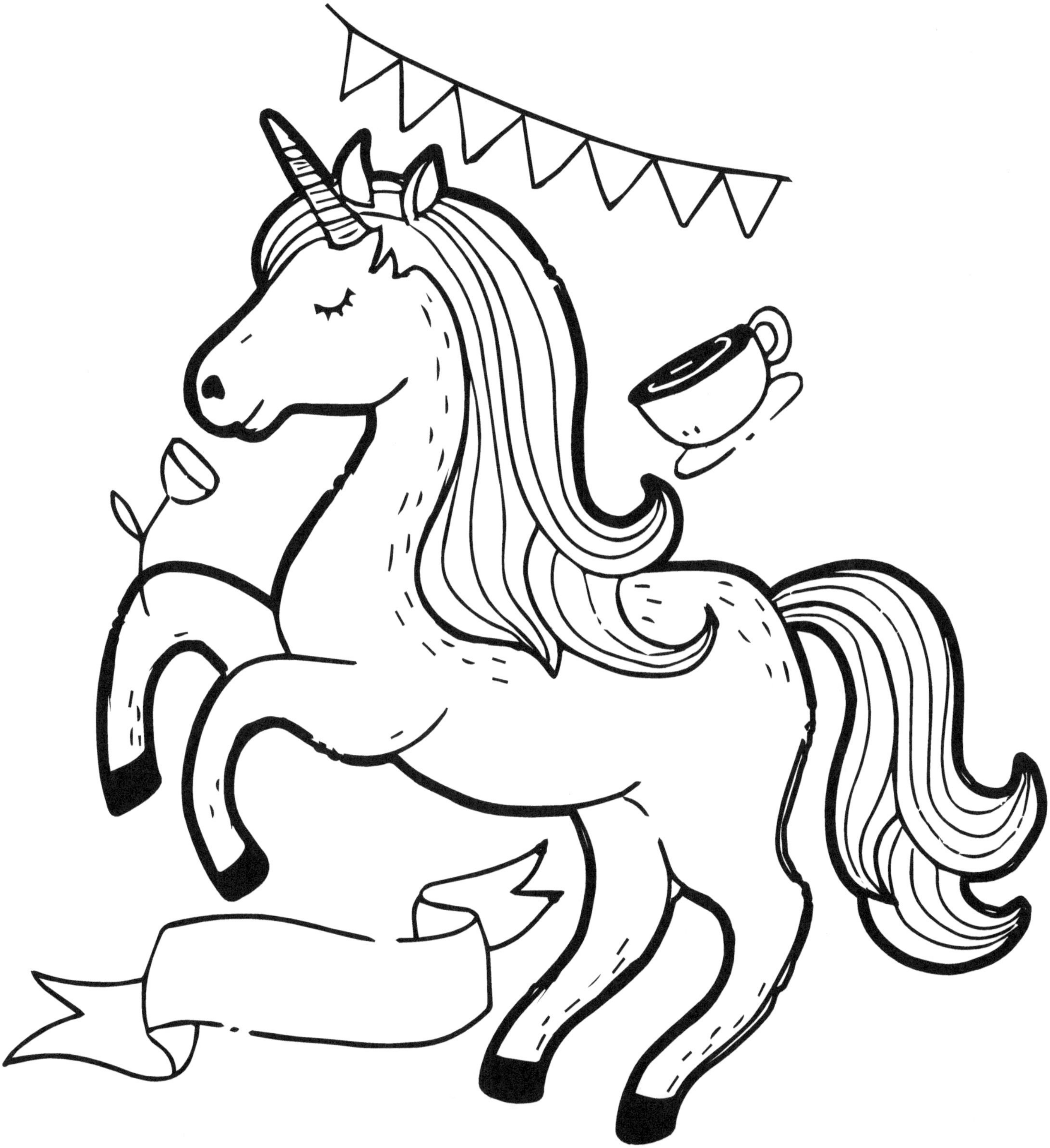

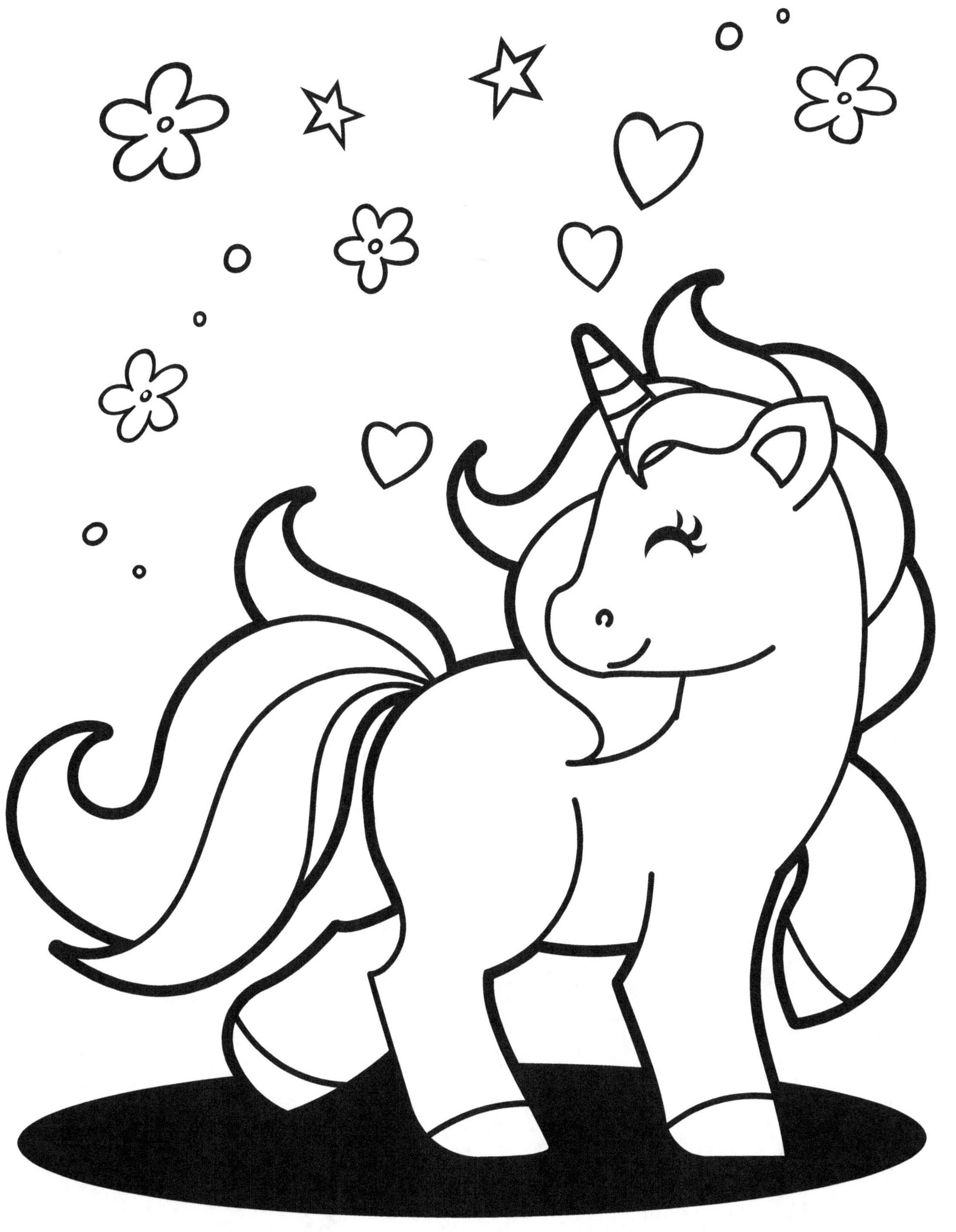

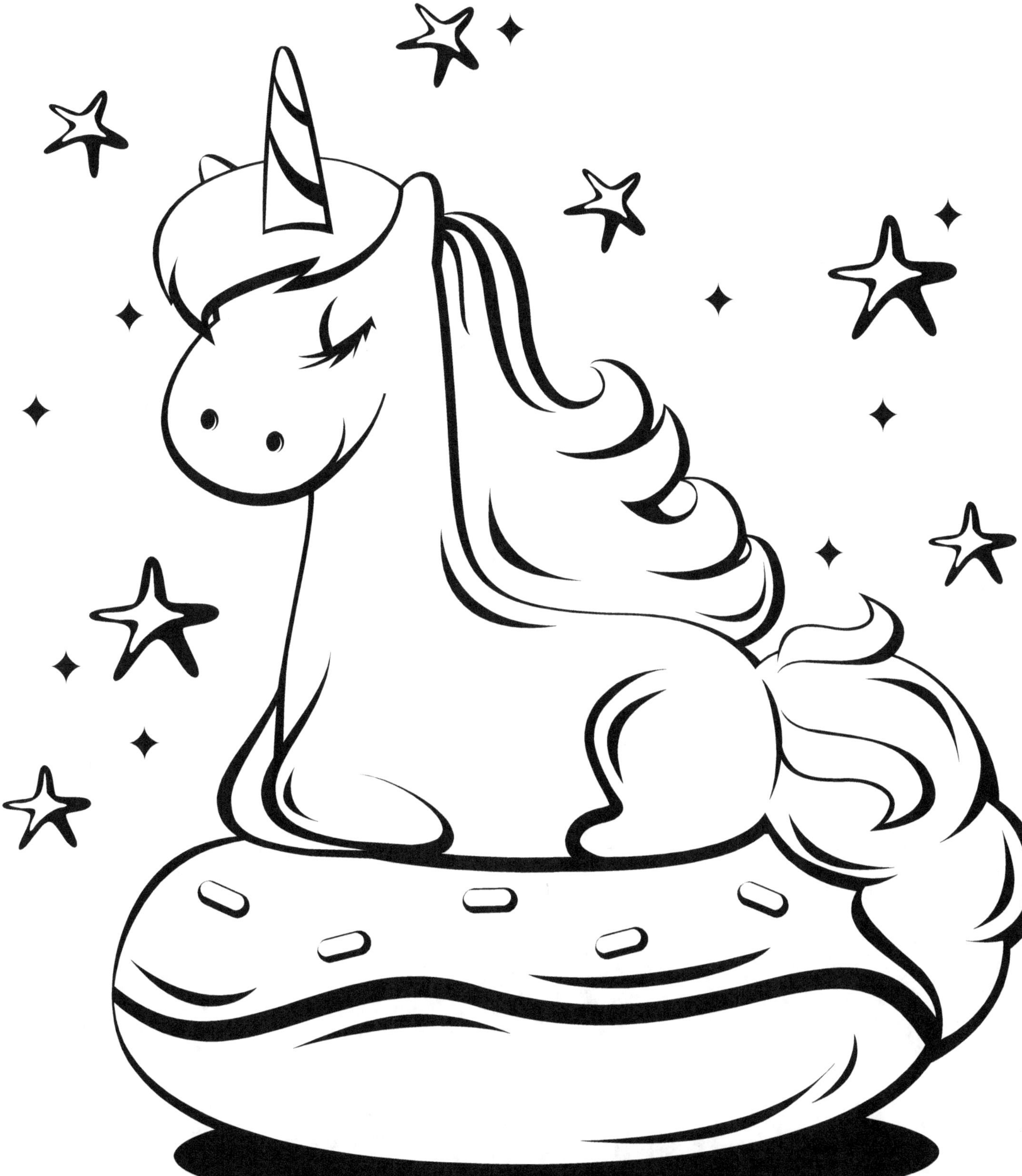

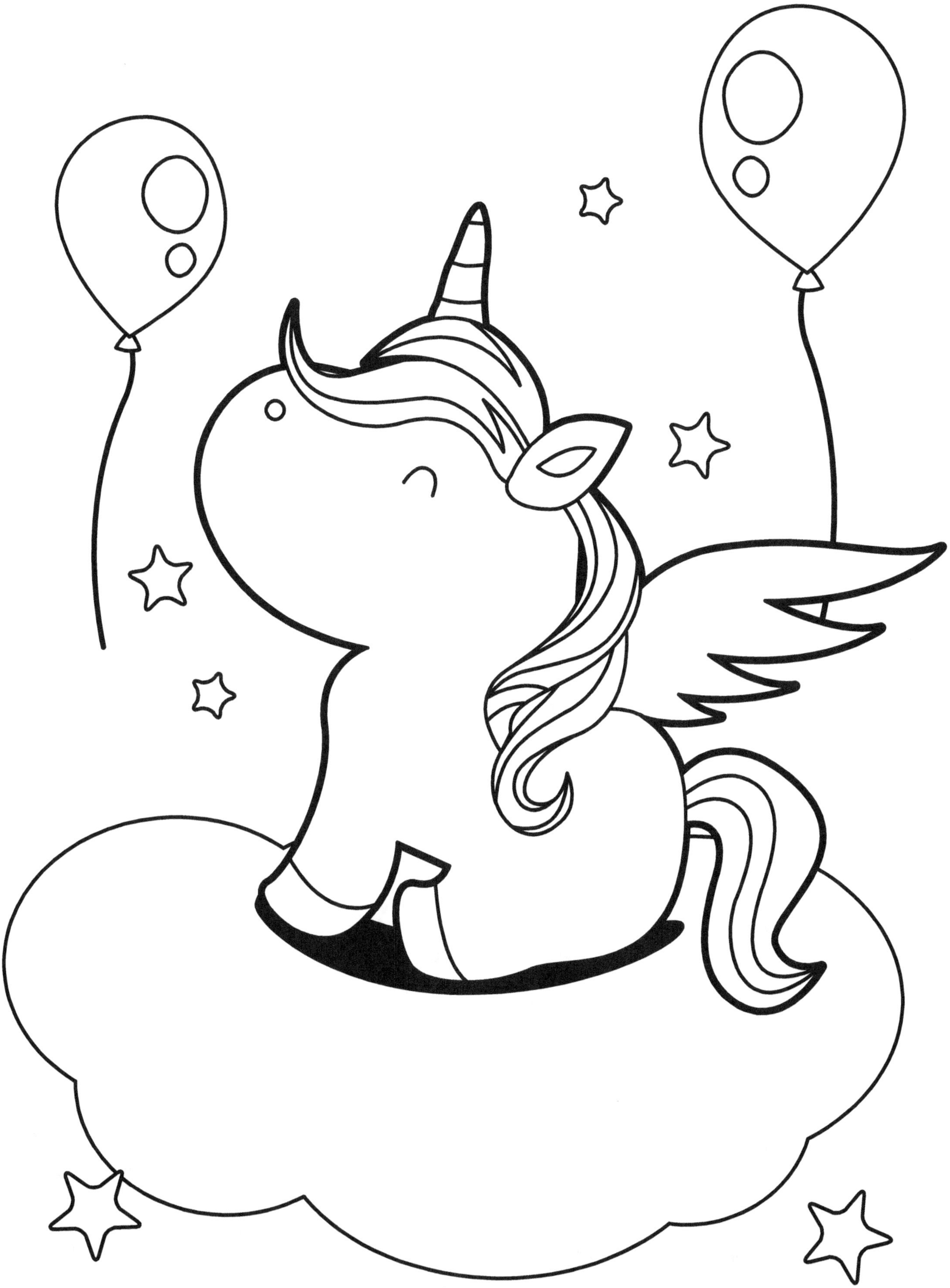

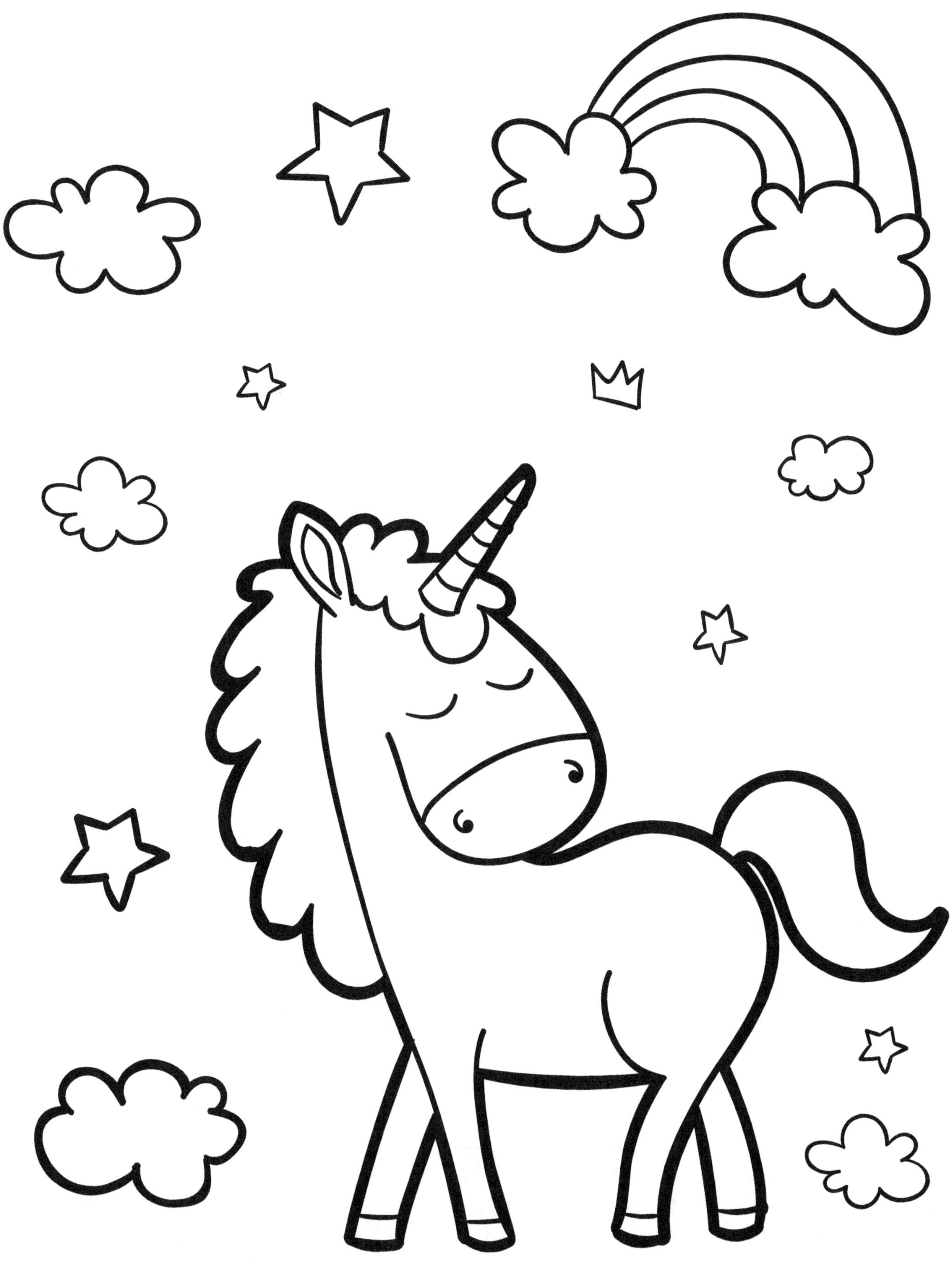

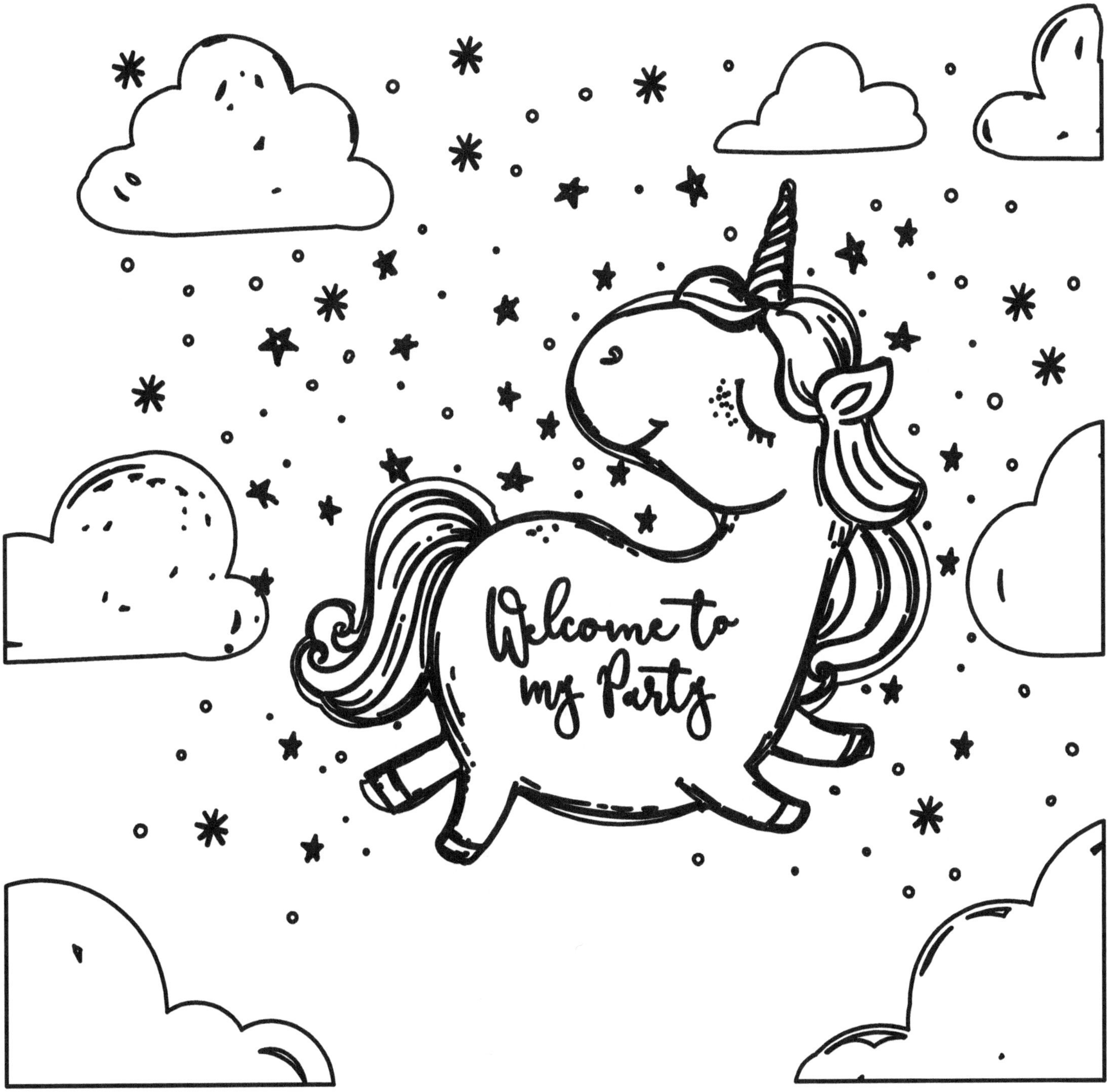
Welcome to
my Party

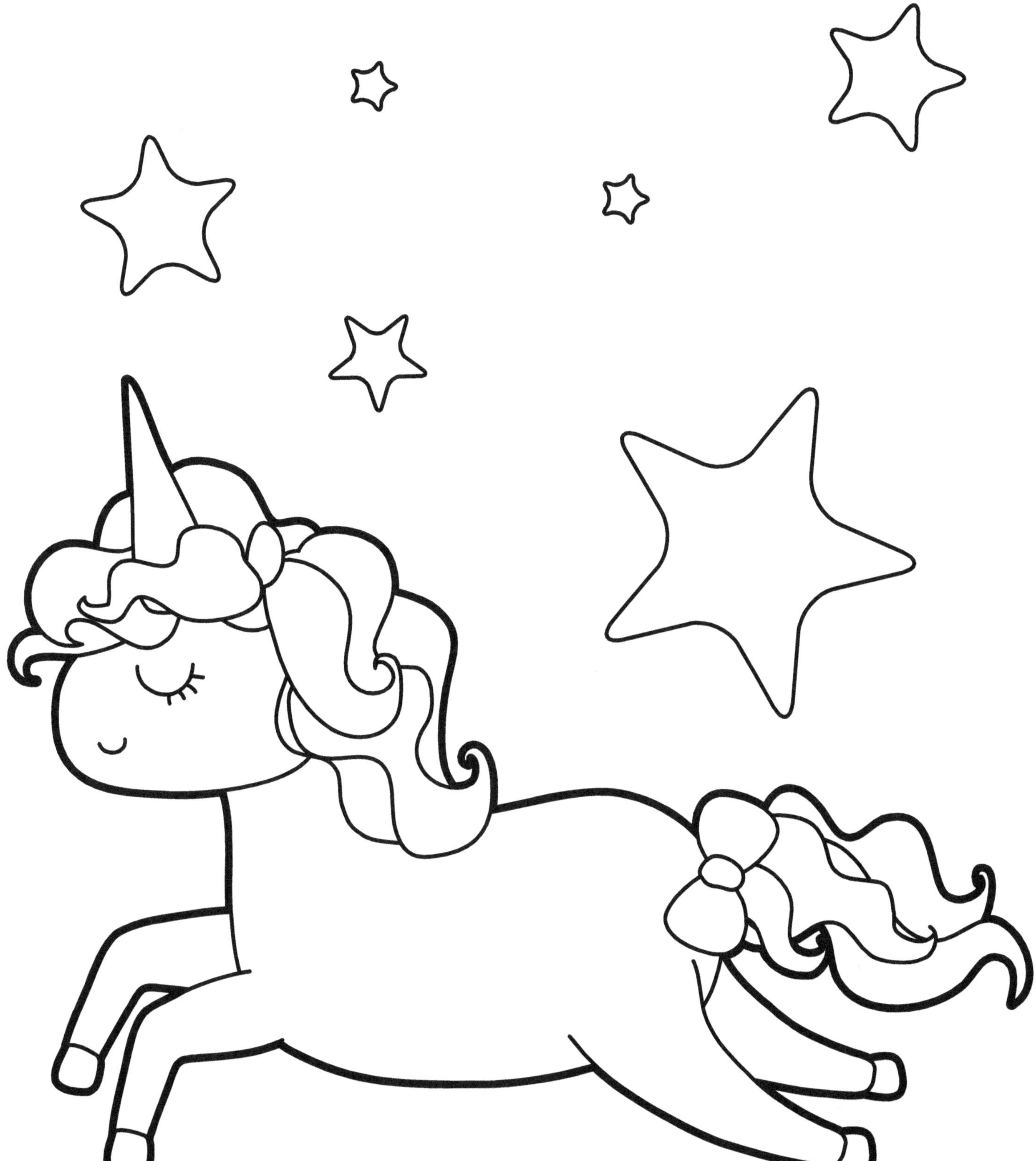

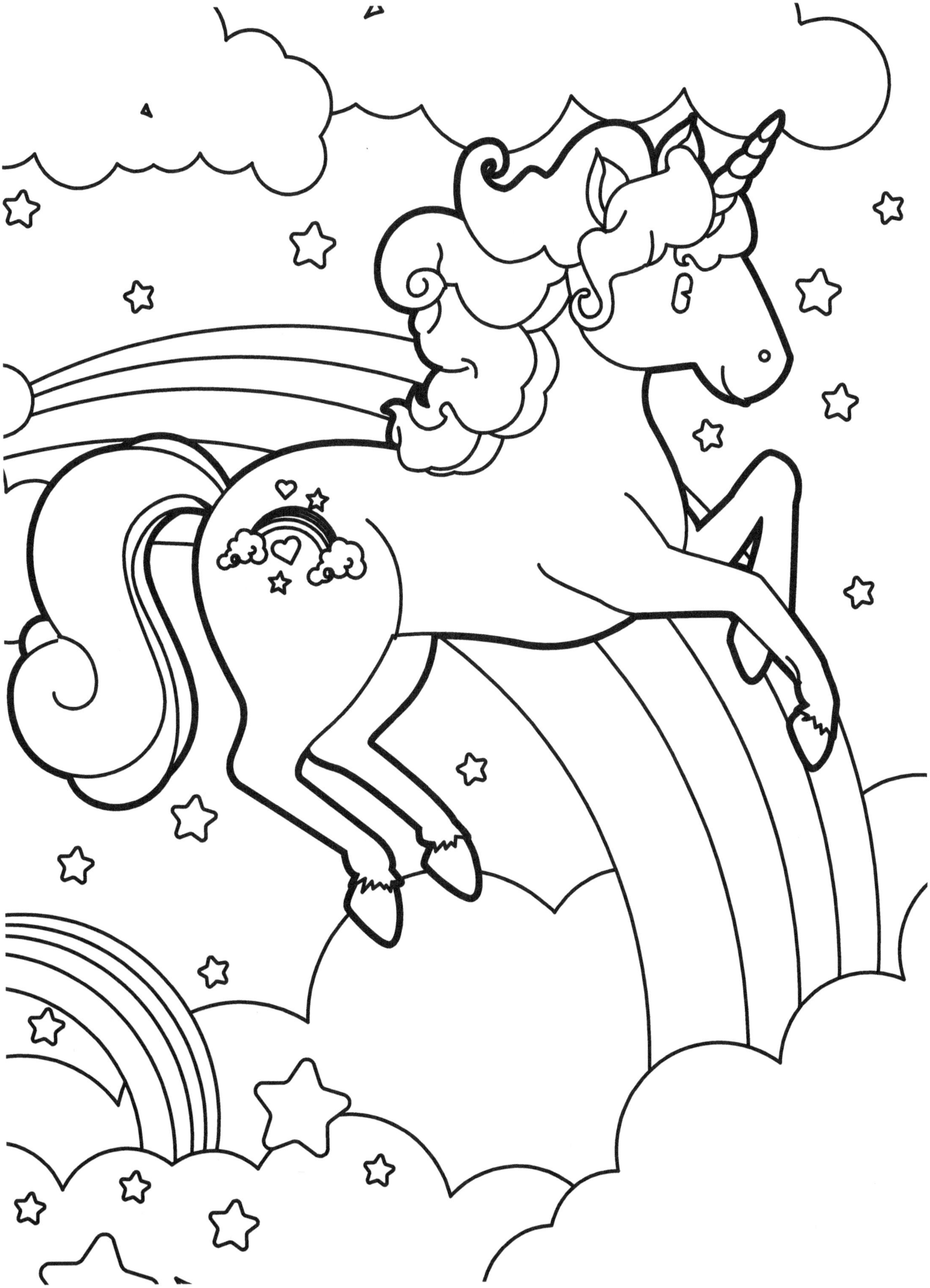

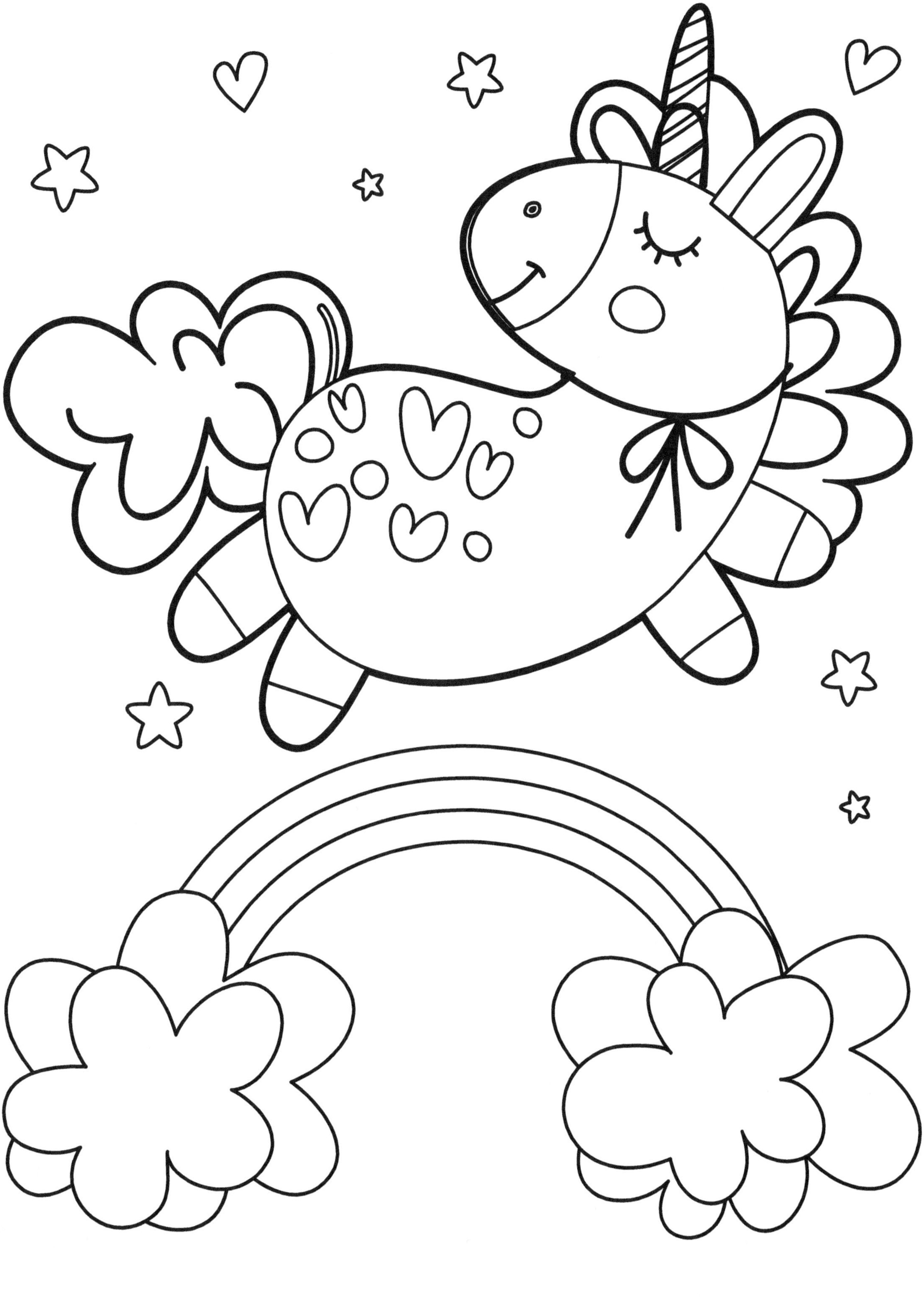

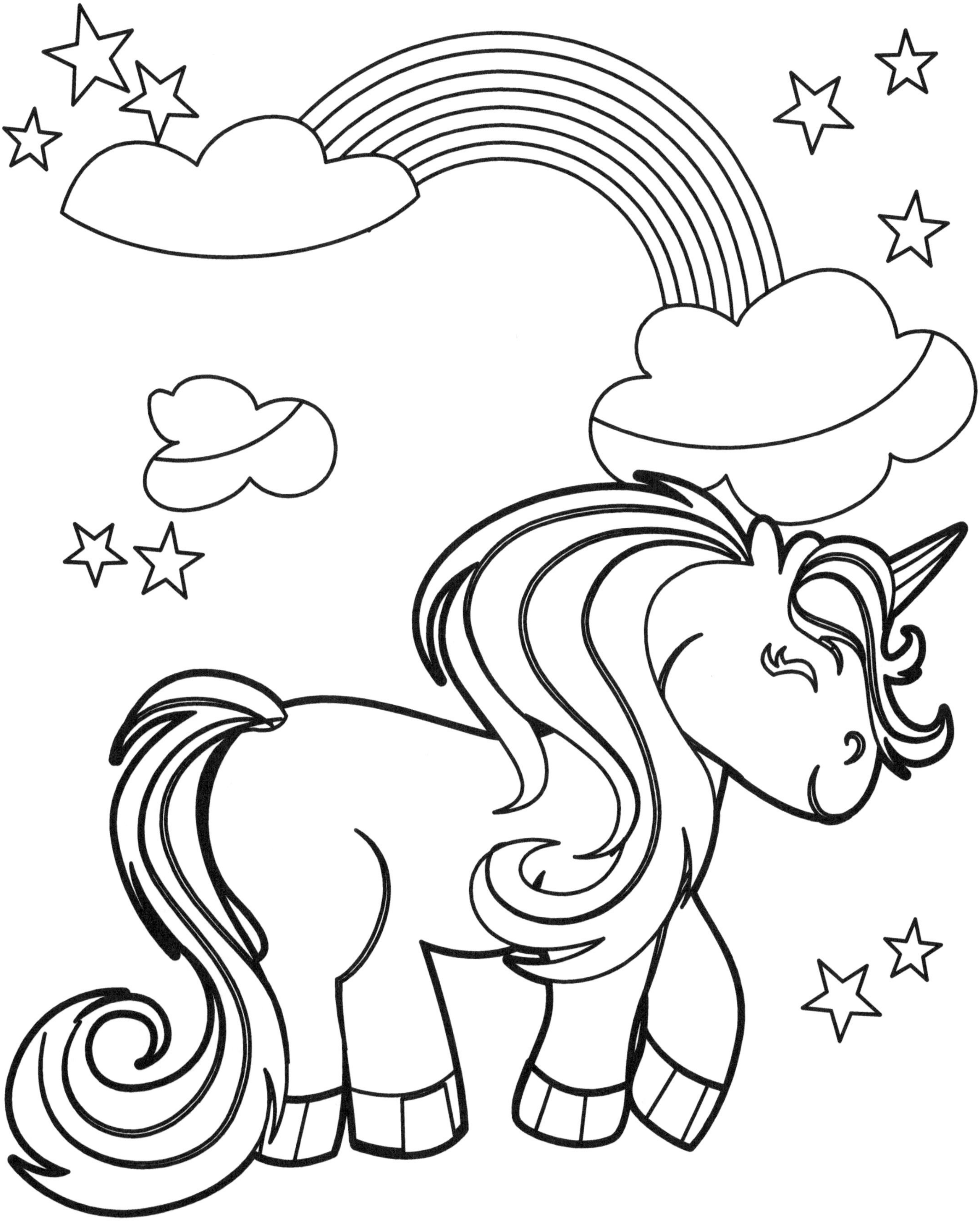

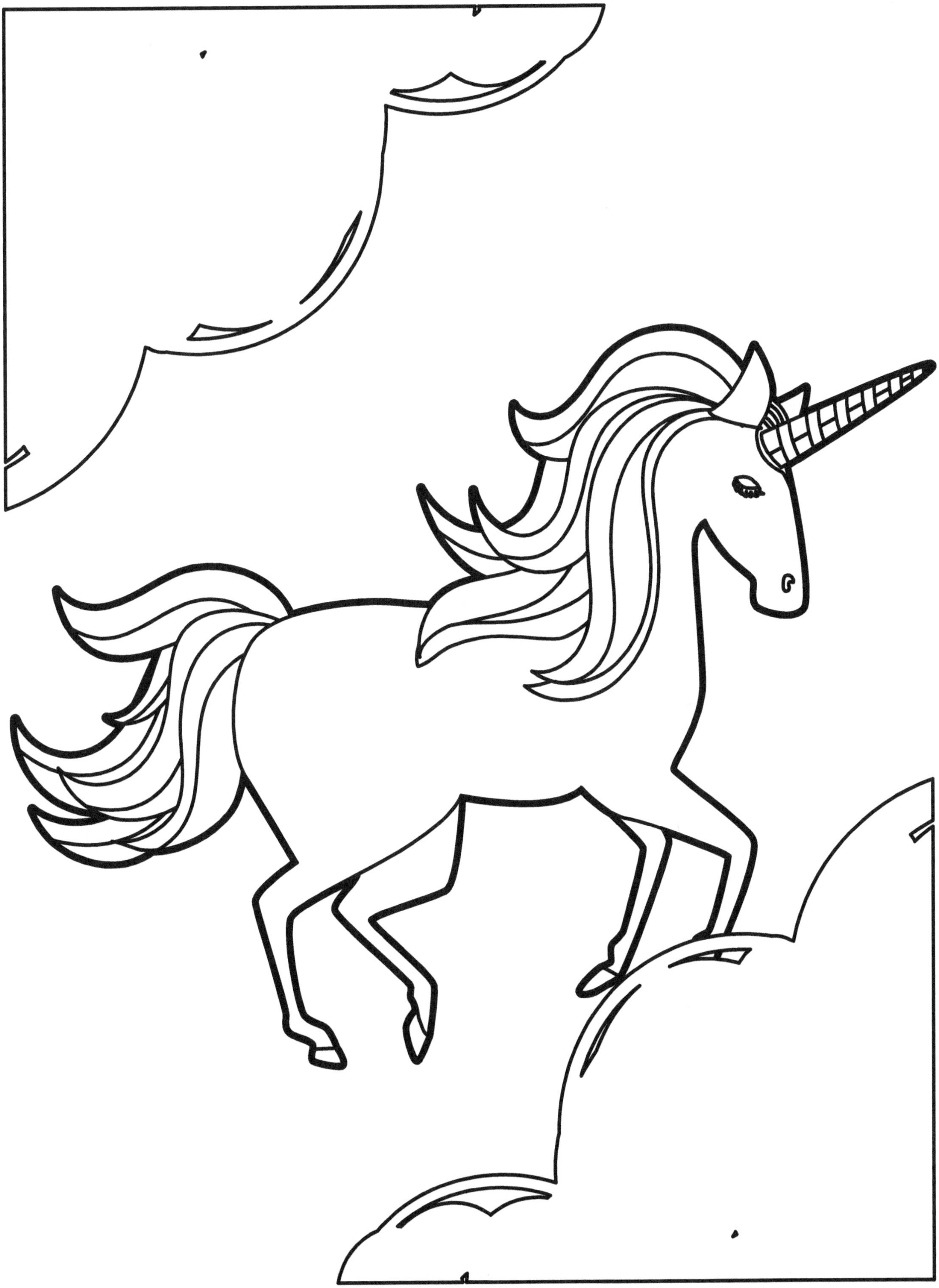

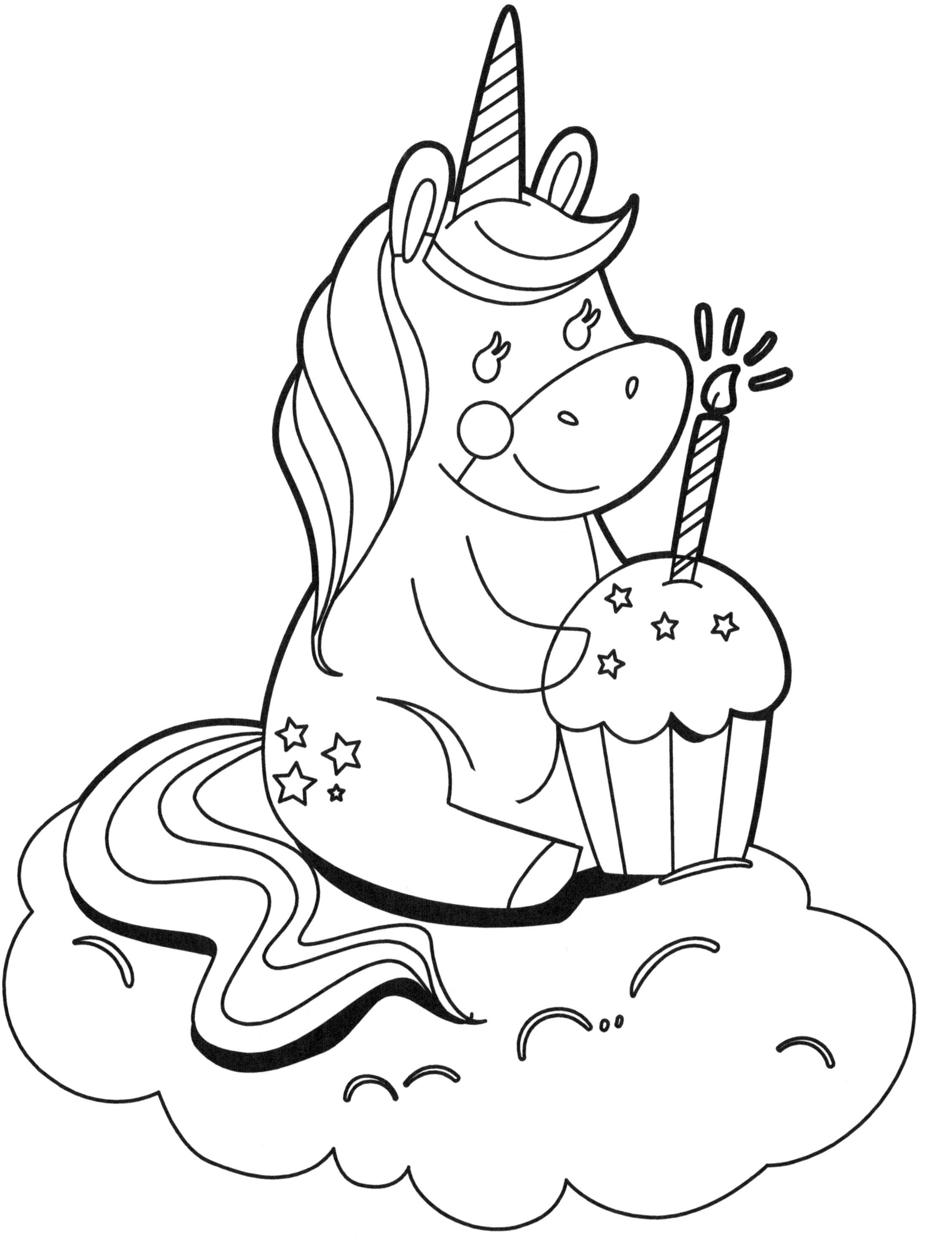

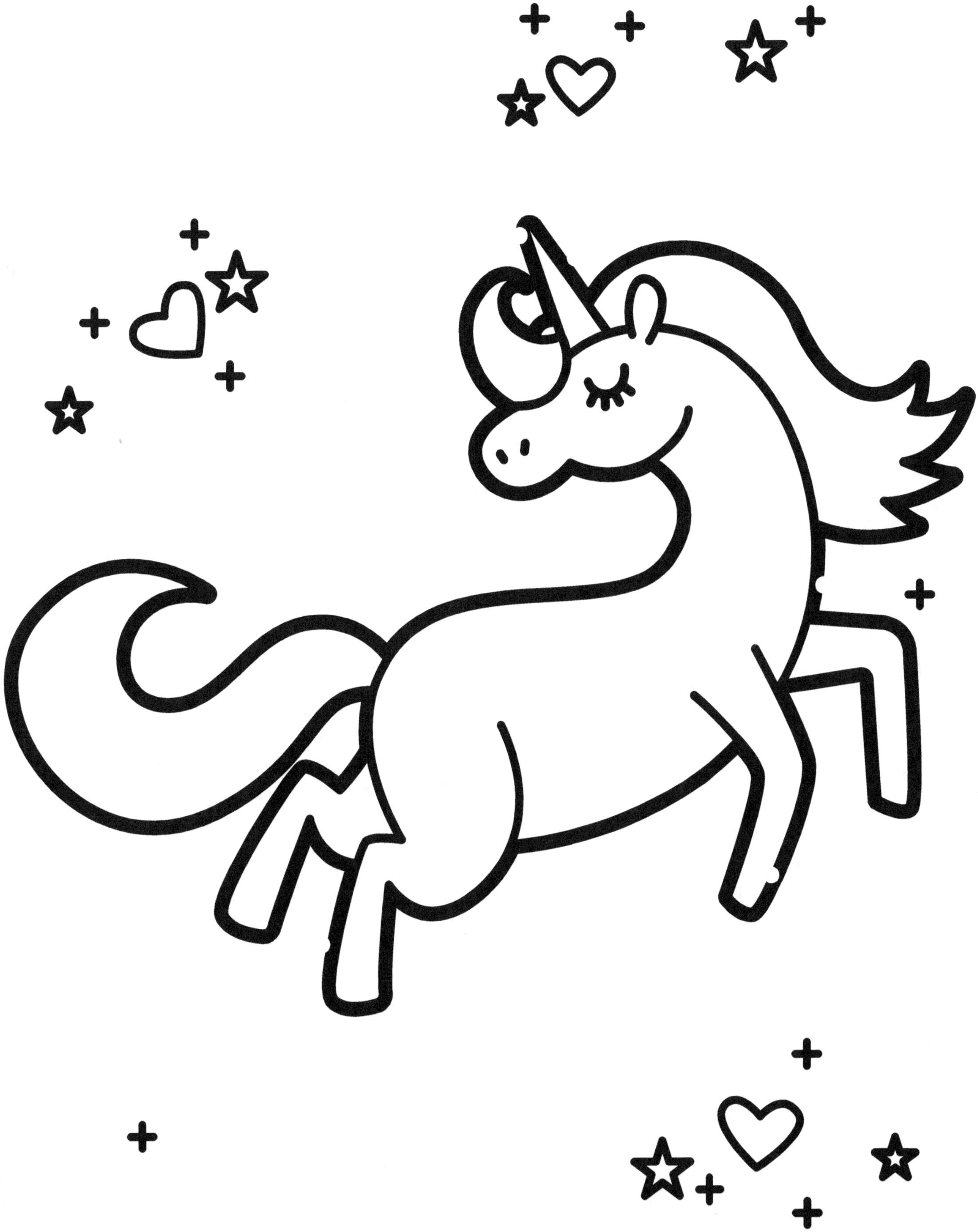

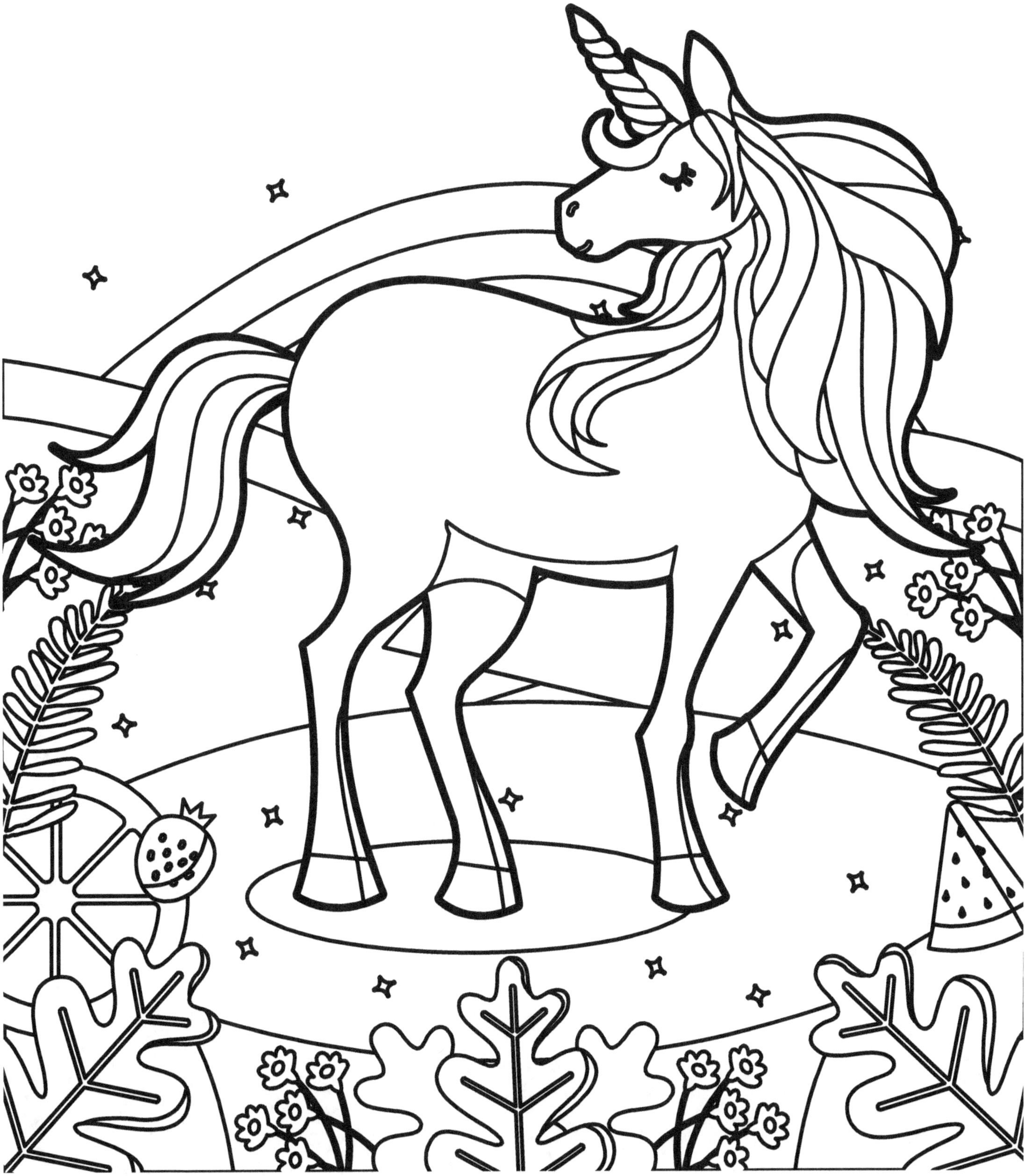

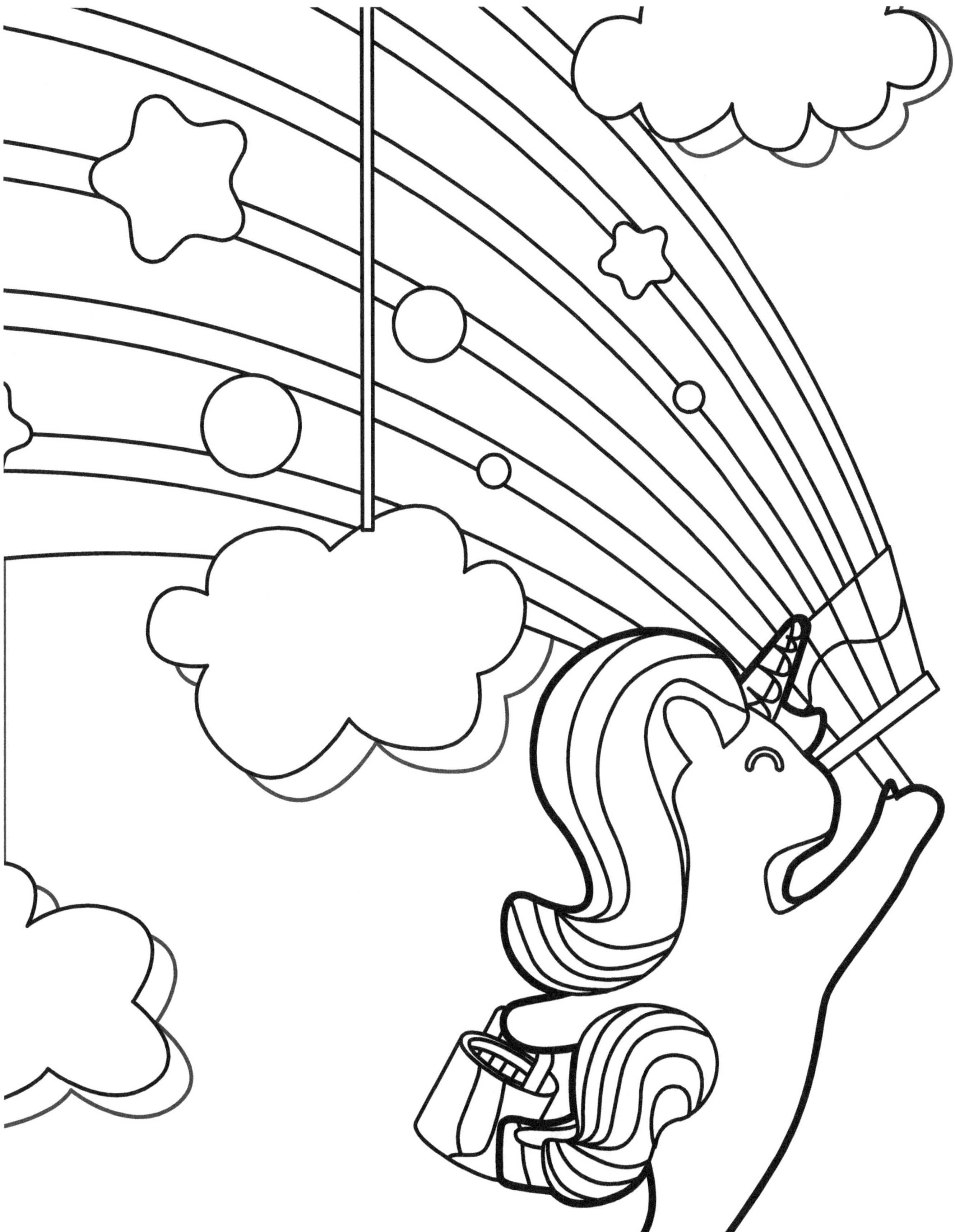

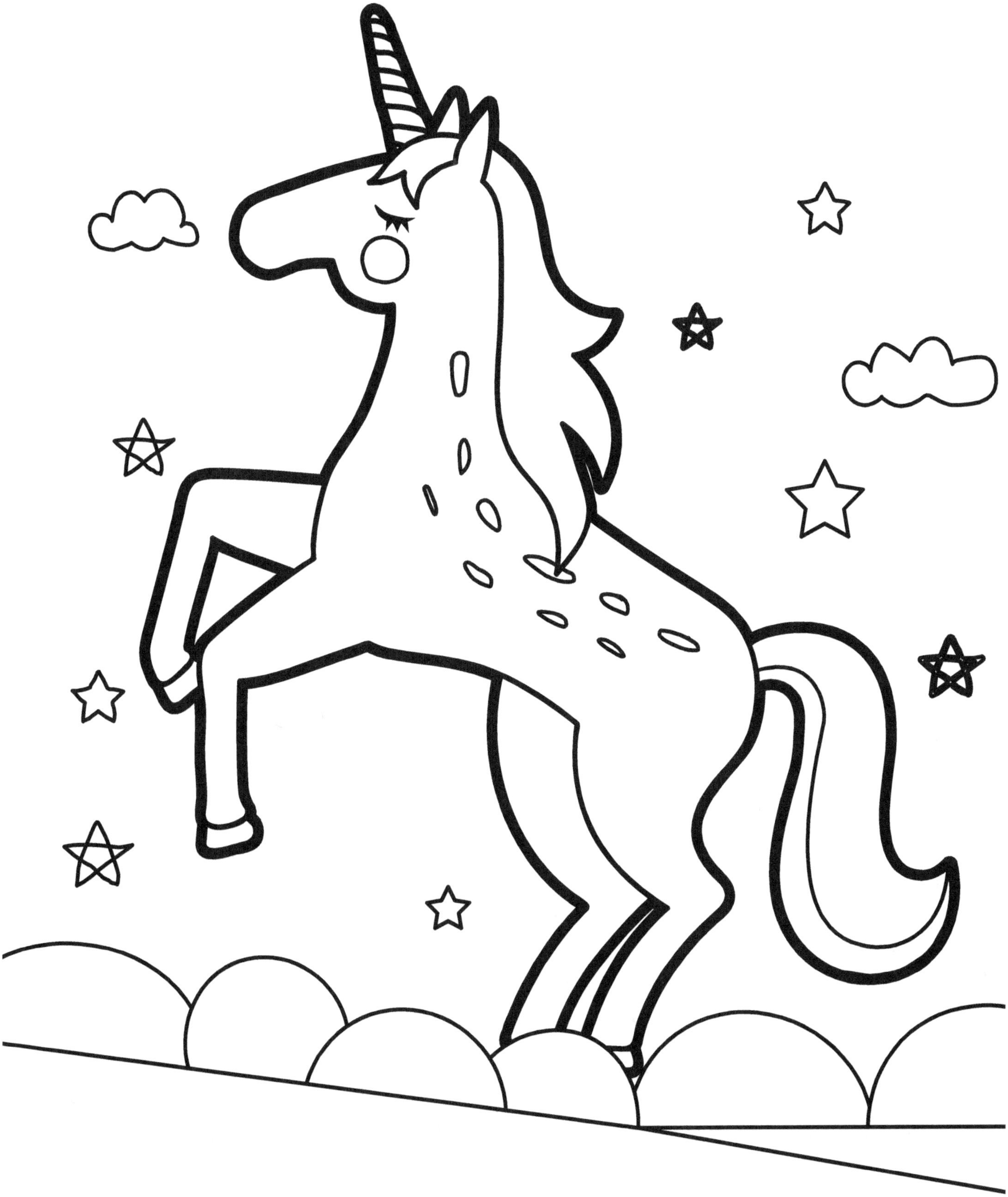

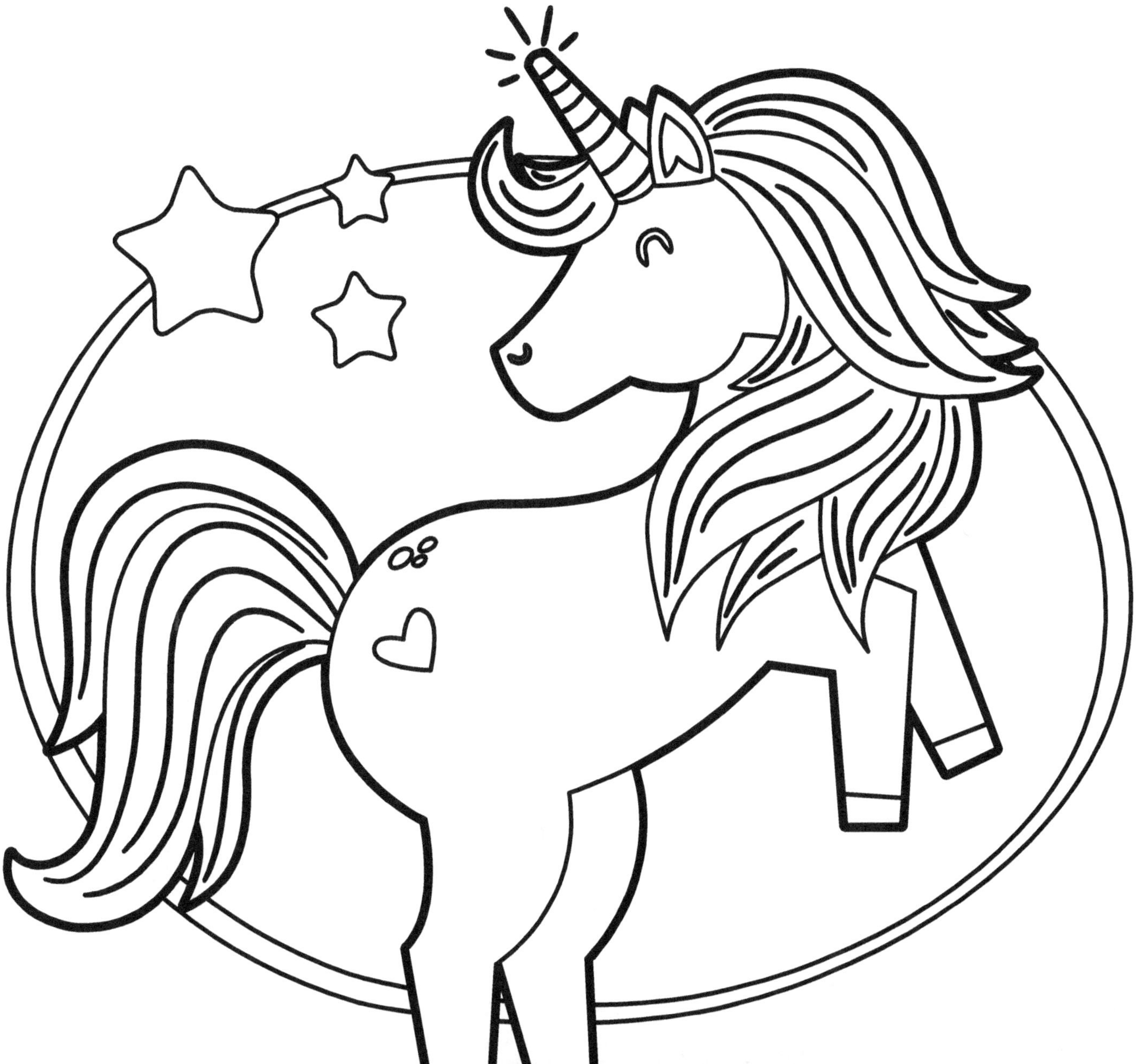

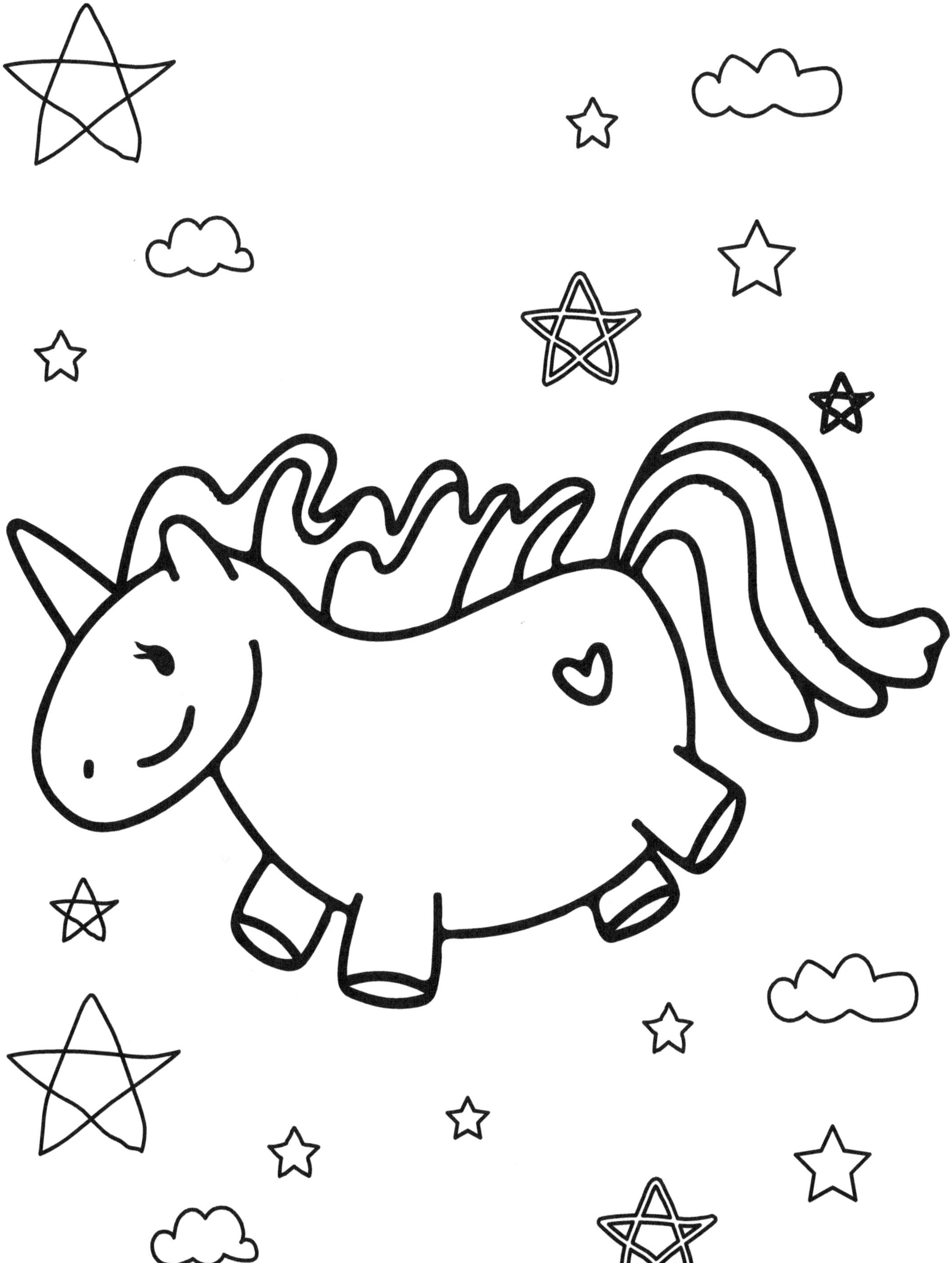

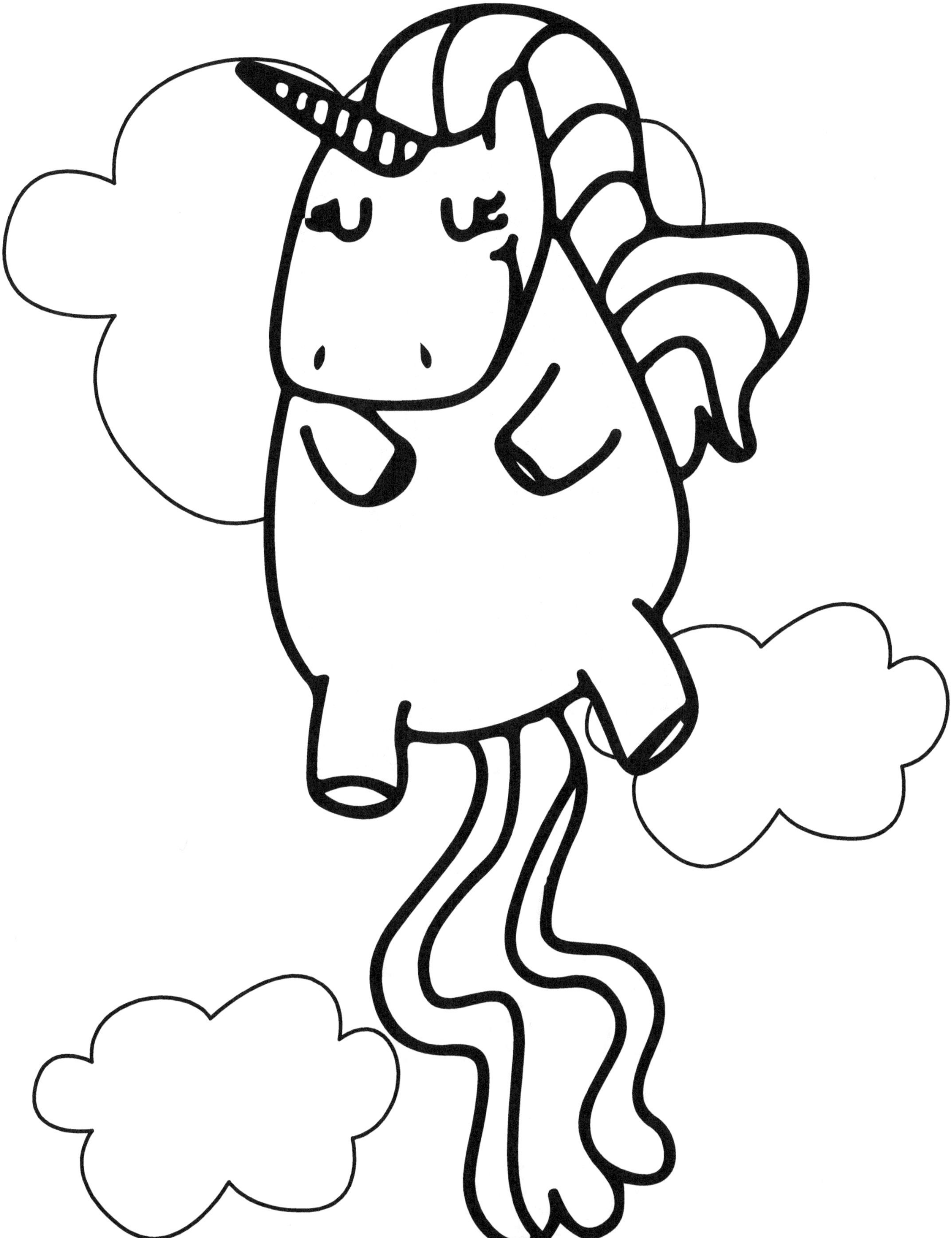

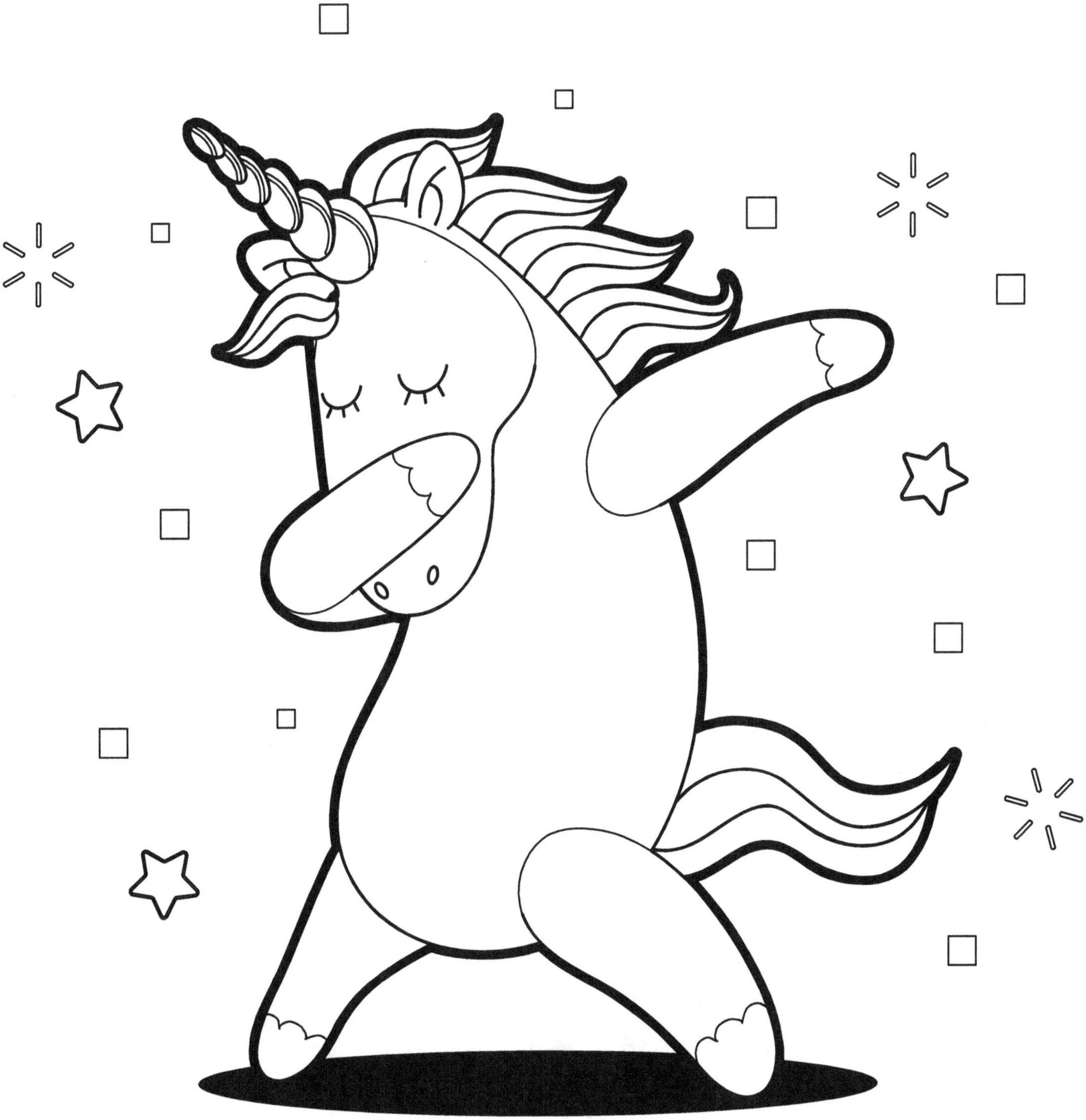

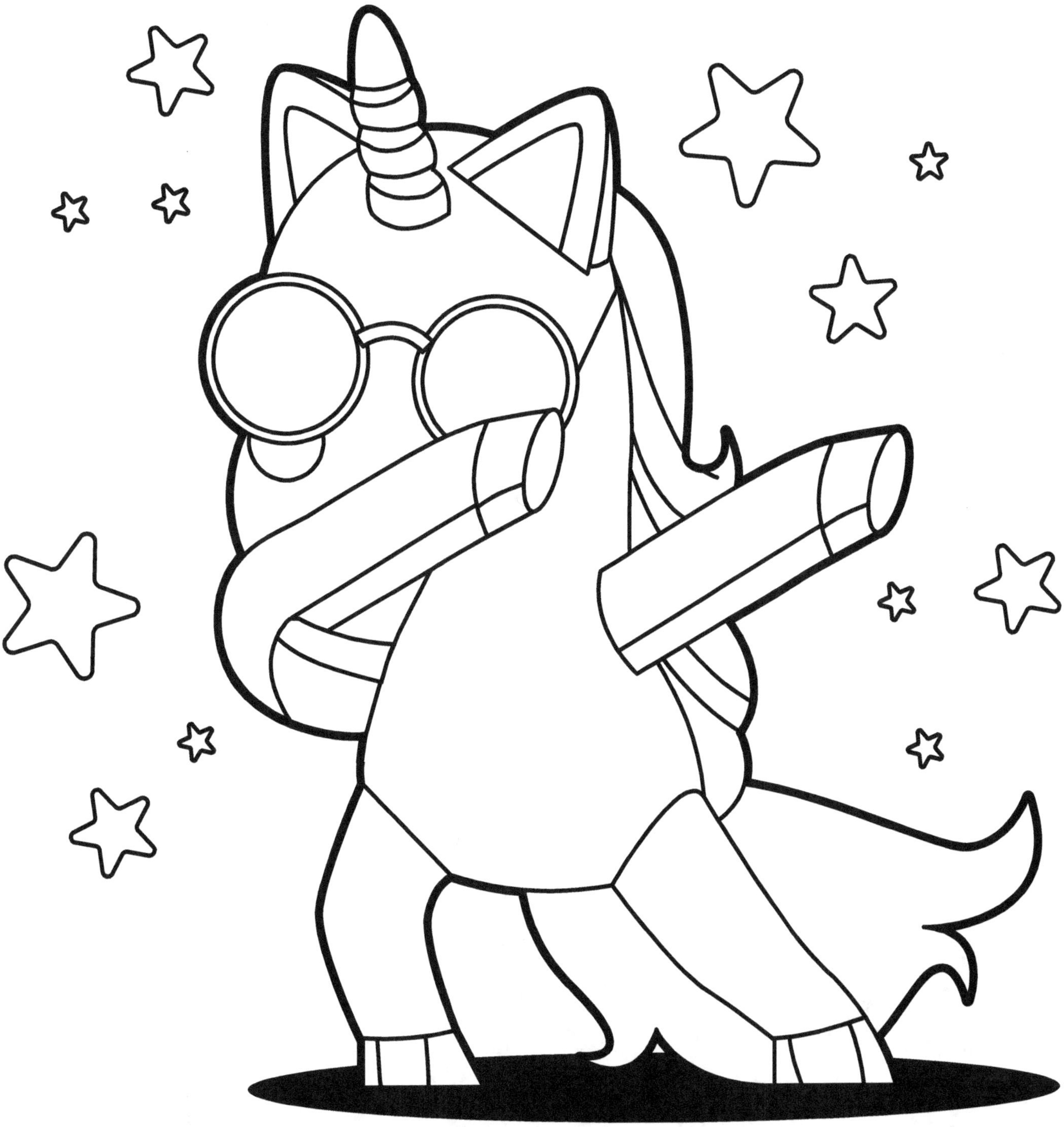

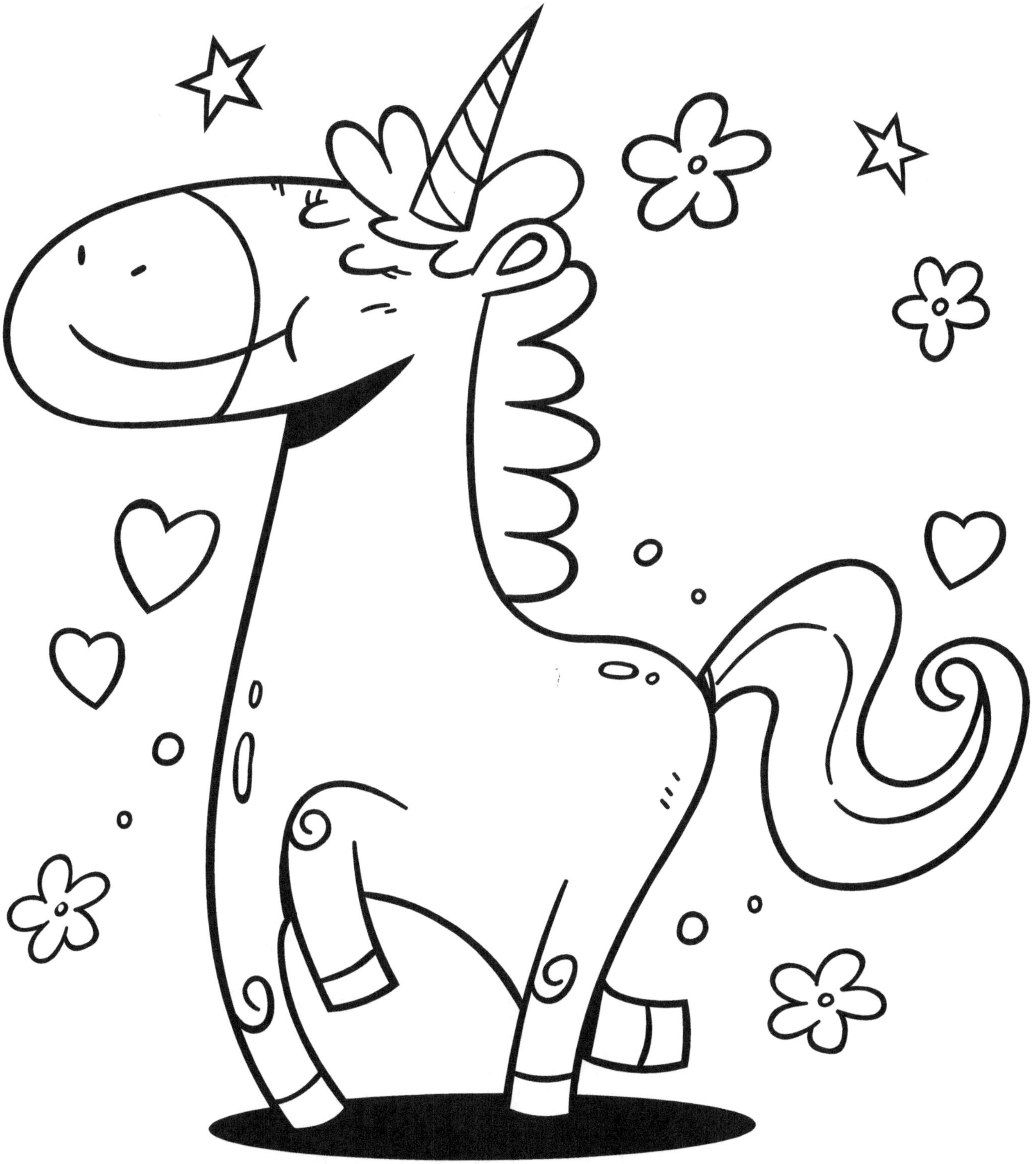

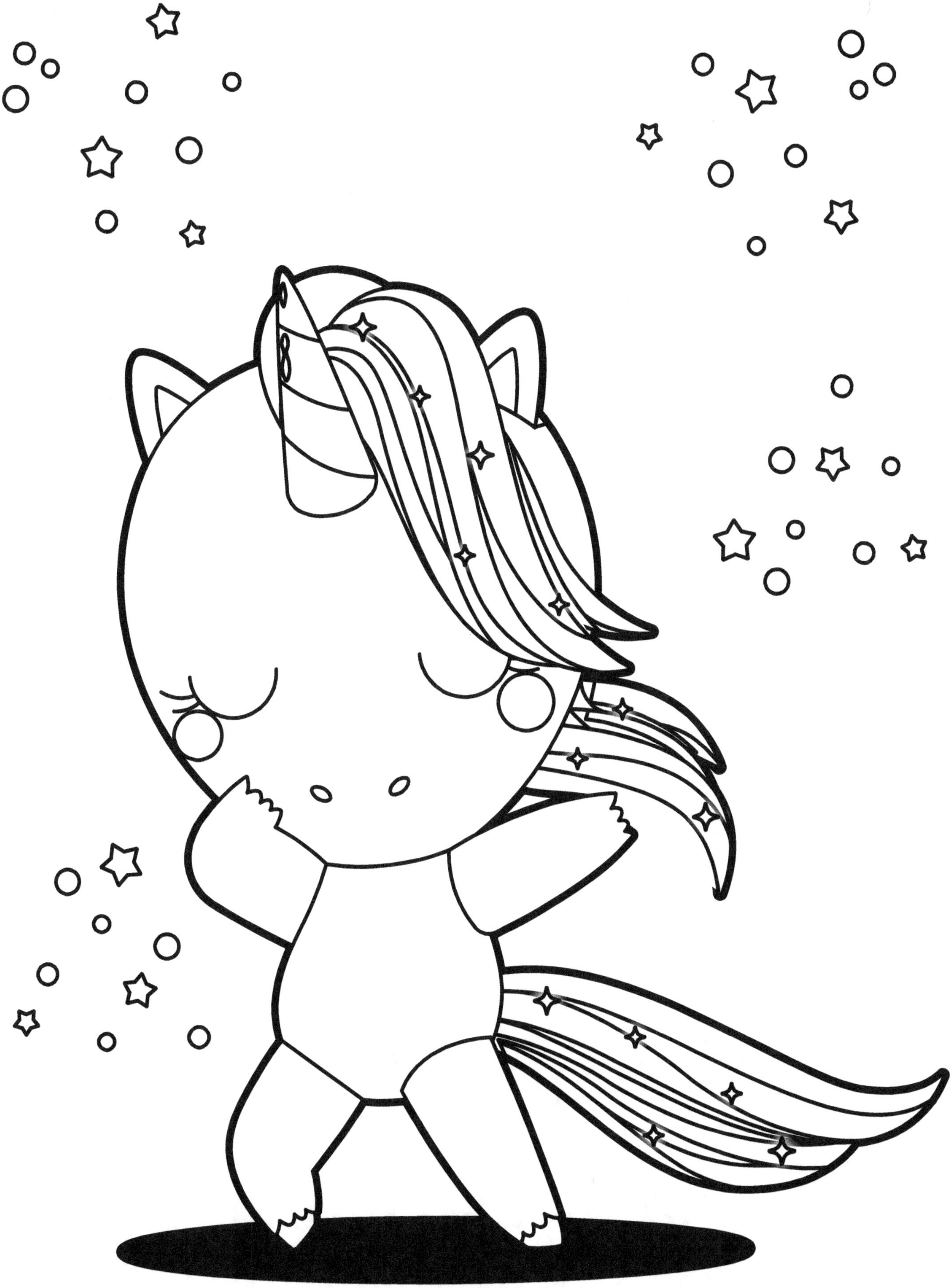

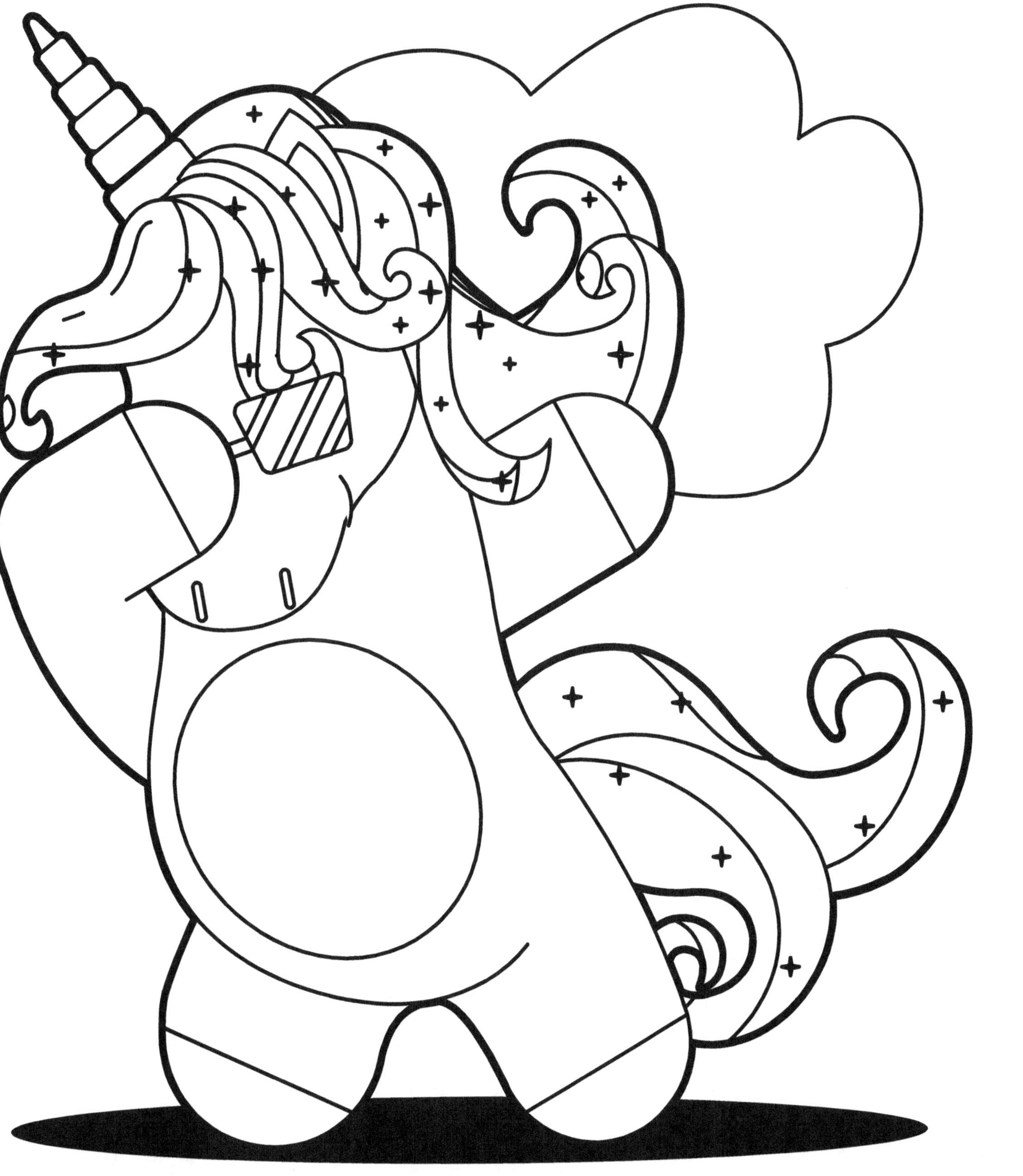

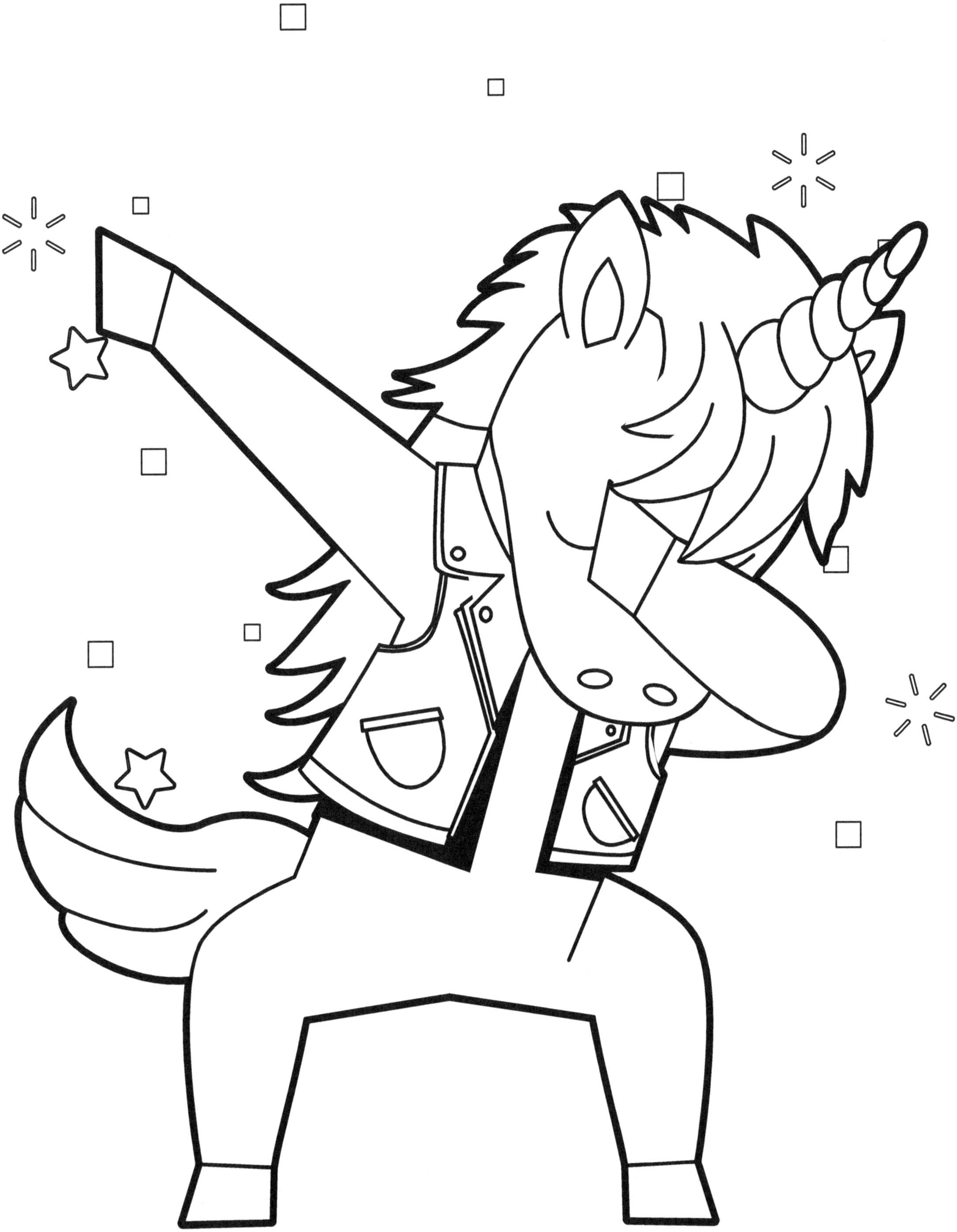

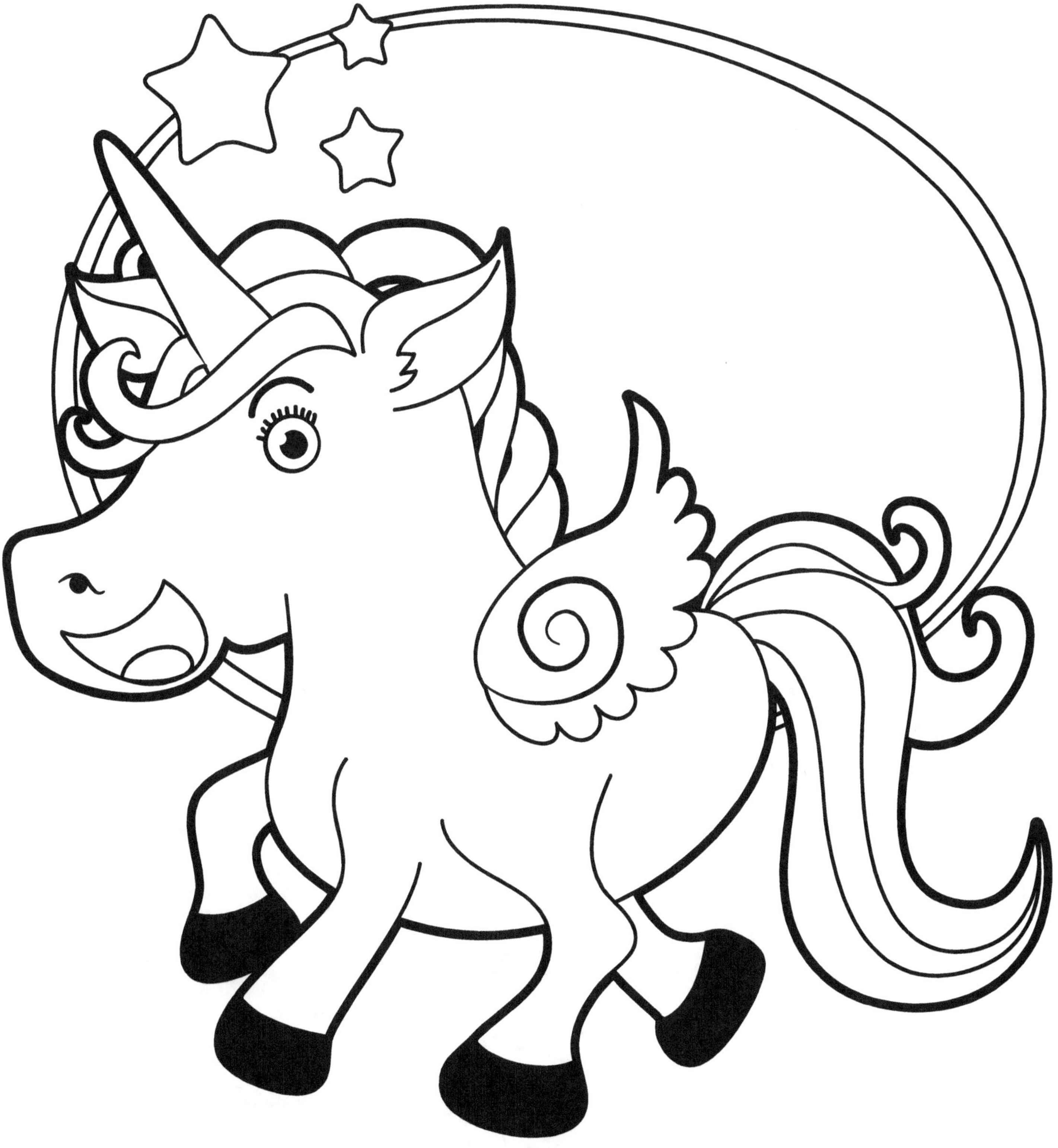

www.ingramcontent.com/pod-product-compliance
Lightning Source LLC
Chambersburg PA
CBHW062336220526
45469CB00008B/2743
* 9 7 8 1 7 2 7 4 0 4 5 7 9 *